Exemplar Series
Grades 6–8

Exemplar Series
Grades 6–8

Edited by
Miles Myers
and Elizabeth Spalding

National Council of Teachers of English
1111 W. Kenyon Road, Urbana, IL 61801-1096

Grateful acknowledgment is made to the following publishers and agencies for permission to use materials from their publications:

Pages 2–21: From *Writing Achievement of California Eighth Graders: Year Two* (1987–88 Annual Report); *Writing Assessment Handbook: Grade 8* (1990); and *A Sampler of English- Language Arts Assessment: Middle Grades* (1994). Permission granted by the California Department of Education.

Pages xii–xiii and 22–27: From *NAEP 1992 Writing Report Card,* by Arthur N. Applebee, Judith A. Langer, Ina V. S. Mullis, Andrew S. Latham, and Claudia A. Gentile (Report No. 23-W01, June 1994); *Reading Assessment Redesigned: Authentic Texts and Innovative Instruments in NAEP's 1992 Survey,* by Judith A. Langer, Jay R. Campbell, Susan B. Neuman, Ina V. S. Mullis, Hilary R. Persky, and Patricia L. Donahue (Report No. 23-FR-07, January 1995); and *Grammar, Punctuation, and Spelling: Controlling the Conventions of Written English at Ages 9, 13, and 17,* by Arthur N. Applebee, Judith A. Langer, and Ina V. S. Mullis (Report No. 15–W03, June 1987). NAEP is a congressionally mandated project of the National Center for Education Statistics of the U.S. Department of Education. NAEP reports are prepared for the Office of Educational Research and Improvement of the U.S. Department of Education by the Educational Testing Service, Princeton, New Jersey, under contract with the National Center for Education Statistics.

Pages 28–31: "My Friend, Albert Einstein," by Banesh Hoffmann, reprinted by permission of Laurence D. Hoffmann.

Page 49: Rubric for breadth of reading adapted from *New Standards 1995–96: Middle Grades English Language Arts Portfolio* (1995) with the permission of the New Standards™.

Pages 53–56: Graphic organizers from Irwin-Devitis, L., & Pease, D. (1995). Using graphic organizers for learning and assessment in middle level classrooms. *Middle School Journal 26*(5), 57–64. Reprinted with permission.

Pages 57 and 58: Graphic organizers reprinted by permission of the author from *Seeking Diversity: Language Arts with Adolescents,* by Linda Rief (Portsmouth, N.H.: Heinemann, 1992).

Page 84: "Narrative Feedback Form" reprinted by permission of Shelby Wolf and Meryl Gearhart.

Book Coordinator: Maria Drees

NCTE Stock Number: 47003

It is the policy of NCTE in its journals and other publications to provide a forum for the open discussion of ideas concerning the content and the teaching of English and the language arts. Publicity accorded to any particular point of view does not imply endorsement by the Executive Committee, the Board of Directors,or the membership at large, except in announcements of policy, where such endorsement is clearly specified.

Although every attempt is made to ensure accuracy at the time of publication, NCTE cannot guarantee that published electronic mail addresses are current.

Library of Congress Cataloging-in-Publication Data
Myers, Miles.
    Exemplar series / Miles Myers and Elizabeth Spalding.
       p.   cm.
     ISBN 0–8141–4698–8 (v. 1 : pbk.). —ISBN 0–8141–4700–3 (v. 2 : pbk.). — ISBN 0–8141–4701–1 (v. 3 : pbk.)
     1. Language arts—Ability testing—United States. 2. English language—Ability testing—United States. 3. Portfolios in education—United States. 4. Language arts—Standards—United States. I. Spalding, Elizabeth, 1951– . II. Title.
LB1576.M943   1997
    428'.0076—dc21
96-47771
CIP

Contents

Foreword

Are you looking for some way to show your students your goals and standards? This book will help you do that and more. The contents of this book grew out of the work of thousands of classroom teachers across the country who worked together to design on-demand tasks and portfolios to assess, among other things, the contents of the *Standards for the English Language Arts* (SELA), which were formulated by the National Council of Teachers of English and the International Reading Association.

The first key point to be made here is that this publication has been a large-group effort. Except for the introduction and some editing work on task descriptions, rubrics, and commentaries, the authors have been largely traffic engineers. The on-demand tasks and portfolio entries selected for this publication were originally developed by teachers working in various state projects (e.g., California, Kentucky), in various national assessment projects (College Board, National Assessment of Educational Progress), and in various curriculum projects sponsored by NCTE. Teachers who have worked in these projects will find that their original work has been modified or added to during the review and piloting process.

The second key point is that the on-demand tasks and portfolios in this publication were selected because they clearly illustrated in some way how the standards for the English language arts appear in typical classroom assignments and typical student performance. The tasks were often selected because they focused on frequently assigned literary selections and frequently assigned writing topics. Some of these tasks and portfolio entries have been "standard" for two dozen years, and some have become "standard" in recent years. The on-demand tasks and portfolio entries were also selected because the student performance, although not the very best or the very worst, was representative of the range from high to low.

The third key point is that the selections presented here are a limited sample of what is needed to assess the content of English language arts. The assessment of the standards for the English language arts requires a wide range of information—on-demand tasks, portfolio entries, multiple-choice tests, and teacher judgments of discussions and oral presentations. Multiple-choice tests and teacher judgments of discussions and oral presentations are not presented in this publication. This publication displays responses to on-demand tasks—the exemplars in the first section—and portfolio entries at different levels in the second section. On-demand tasks are assignments used across many classrooms, almost always with time limitations, and the portfolios are a combination of assigned and freely chosen projects, timed and untimed. On-demand tasks focus on particular standards and allow us to make comparisons across classes and districts. Portfolio entries usually tell us something unique about how each student achieves the English standards, providing evidence of how a student develops an idea over time, how several performances interact, how the student reflects about his or her work, and what the student emphasizes when allowed to make choices. We hope both exemplars and portfolios will illuminate further the processes involved in achieving the NCTE/IRA standards and contribute to the ongoing conversations these standards have initiated.

Introduction

The NCTE/IRA standards for the English language arts have three interrelated parts: (1) the content standards themselves; (2) descriptions of classroom practice, or the *Standards in Practice* series; and (3) performance standards, or the *Exemplar Series*. In addition, NCTE and IRA have together published a statement on principles of assessment (*Standards for the Assessment of Reading and Writing*, IRA/NCTE, 1994). This book is one of the three books in the *Exemplar Series* and is intended for those who have wondered how teachers rank student work or how teachers have translated English language arts standards into student performance. This book will provide examples of both rankings of student work and translations of the English standards (NCTE/IRA, 1996) into student performances.

Two approaches are now used in the United States to describe content standards and performance standards — specification and exemplification. In specification, content standards and levels of performance are described by small bits of behavior from one part of the language system. Usually these specifications are sequenced by grade level. This model for content standards and performance standards is very popular among policy-makers and op-ed writers because it simplifies the world and makes the adoption of standards seem easy. The answers are right or wrong, and the sequence is certain. For example, one state has mandated in its content standards that "modifiers" be taught in the elementary grades, that pronoun case be taught in middle school, and that pronoun reference be taught in high school. Clearly, however, "modifiers" and the other parts of the language system are learned throughout the grades, not just in one. Another state wants the use of commas in a series taught in one grade, and commas for nonrestrictive clauses or phrases taught in another. These sequences never work in the classroom. Why? Many reasons. For one thing, one part of the language system influences others. For example, the use of particular phrase and clause modifiers produces new problems in punctuation.

Although specification will not work to produce a list of content standards, specification will work to identify parts of the performance standards assessing the content. Some knowledge in English language arts requires the specification of the names of things, and this kind of knowledge can be assessed with multiple-choice tests, which are good measures of most small-bit specifications. Most national and state programs use these multiple-choice tests and describe the performance levels at each grade level as a given number of right answers. These measures are useful for some purposes, but they have serious limits. We need more emphasis on exemplification in our descriptions of performance levels.

The approach used here to describe performance levels is exemplification. Exemplification is used by the School Curriculum and Assessment Authority of Wales and England, by the National Assessment of Educational Progress (NAEP), by the College Board, and by some states, particularly California, Kentucky, and Vermont, to describe student performance at different levels. Exemplification is not the same as specification, or the one-part-at-a-time/one-error-at-a-time approach. In exemplification, instead of learning one part at a time, students learn one situation at a time in reading, writing, or speaking. Instead of measuring student achievement by the number of right or wrong answers in performance, exemplification uses on-demand exemplars and portfolio entries to describe levels of student achievement in particular tasks. Exemplars show student performance on on-demand tasks covering a range of language situations, and portfolios show student performance on particular tasks over time. Exemplification measures with judgments of the quality of performance in various situations. Student "errors" influence judgments of quality, but counting errors alone is not an adequate measurement of quality in exemplification.

The On-Demand Tasks

Performance on each on-demand task is illustrated by an exemplar. An exemplar is a sample of a student performance on a task in a given situation (i.e., a situation sample), accompanied by a rubric and a commentary on that sample. Thus, in this book, levels of performance are described with (1) a description of the on-demand task, which has been given across many classrooms; (2) grade-level samples of student work on specific on-demand tasks requiring particular kinds of knowledge in English language arts (e.g., writing reports, responding to literature); (3) rubrics describing the different achievement levels for a given task or situation; and (4) commentaries showing the relationship of each sample to the rubric. In general, three achievement levels—high, middle, and low—are presented for each on-demand task. The achievement levels make visible the values and standards that teachers share.

The Portfolios

A portfolio is a collection over time of student performances on classroom assignments. These assignments are tasks showing the student's performance in a range of knowledge domains in English language arts, the student's development throughout the year, and the processes used by students in various tasks. This book presents three portfolios which exemplify achievement on the standards. Each has been ranked at one of three achievement levels: high, middle, or low. For each entry in the portfolio, marginal comments based on a rubric will highlight strengths and weaknesses of that particular piece. Following each portfolio is a summary commentary which links the portfolio as a whole to the rubrics or marginal comments.

The Rubrics

The rubrics that accompany the student samples in the *Exemplar Series* are drawn from several frameworks for assessing student performances in English language arts. Frameworks often focus on reading and writing in general, across purposes and audiences. Rubrics usually focus on particular kinds of writing or particular purposes and audiences. In addition, rubrics usually give general descriptors of several levels of performance. In the *Exemplar Series*, the framework described in this introduction is a general description, and the rubrics are situation-specific and achievement-level-specific.

The Commentaries

In exemplification, a description of an achievement level must have three parts—sample of performance, rubric, and commentary. All three are necessary. The commentary describes the links between rubrics and samples, pointing to specific evidence from the sample and adding evaluations of the overall work.

STANDARDS IN THE CLASSROOM

Standards for the English Language Arts (SELA) tells us that in the classroom we will find (1) students who are playing the roles of readers and writers, discovering how to shape their experience and to connect their experience to text; (2) evidence of public audiences, classroom audiences, and personal audiences playing the roles of reader and responder to student work; (3) subject matter, whether imaginary, public/civic, or academic and informational; (4) different tools (computers, telephones, calculators, faxes) and editing groups; (5) various texts both literary and nonliterary for reading, hearing, and viewing; (6) language reference books on the structure of grammar (phonology, morphology, syntax) and text; and (7) evidence of cognitive and metacognitive development in drafts from editing, discussion, and response groups, including learning logs, outlines, notes, and other forms. On a map, the classroom might look like this:

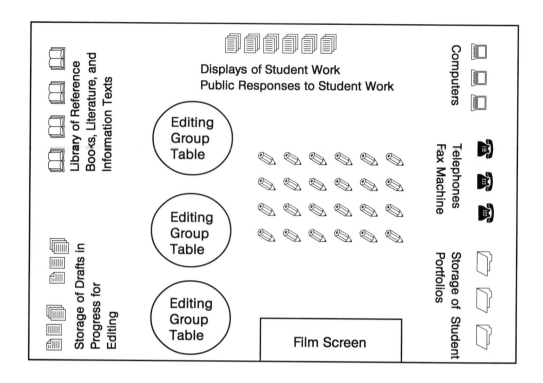

From the student work in this typical classroom, teachers have specified some kinds of performance as particularly salient: (1) narrative writing (writing firsthand reports, autobiography and biography), (2) argumentative writing (editorials, problem solutions, letters to the editor, position statements), (3) report writing (newspaper reports, portraits, information summaries), (4) reading depth—response to literature (character analysis, intertextual comparisons, short story evaluations, summaries), (5) reading depth—response to informational texts (history, general information, bus schedules), (6) reading breadth (reading journals, book logs), and (7) visual representation, including mapping and charts. Each of the three books in this exemplar series (K–5, 6–8, 9–12) includes most of these types, but not necessarily all. These are not the only performances of importance, but they are common performances in English classes and are stressed in *Standards for the English Language Arts.*

A FRAMEWORK FOR ASSESSMENT

What do exemplars and portfolios tell us about what students know? Exemplars and portfolios exhibit the standards in action in three ways of knowing, in four domains of knowledge in English language arts, and in various patterns of student development.

Three Ways of Knowing

The three ways of knowing are, first, declarative knowledge ("knowing that"), including the knowledge usually exhibited by students in traditional tests ("The main character is a spider"); second, procedural, process, or performance knowledge ("knowing how"), including the use of reading strategies, writing strategies, and strategies for turning various kinds of knowledge into action; and third, background or general awareness knowledge, including general awareness of the purposes of language ("knowing about/ why").

I. *Knowing that* is the factual, informational knowledge of English language arts, including information about genre, literary forms, and rules of spelling or punctuation or subject-verb agreement. Knowing that is developed through memorization, reading and rereading again to retain information. Knowing that can often be assessed with multiple-choice tests, but this approach alone is inadequate.

II. *Knowing how* is the procedural or process knowledge of action, of using the four domains of knowledge in an actual situation. One can name the parts of a sentence (knowing that) and still not be able to write one (knowing how). Knowing how requires assessment during the use of language.

III. *Knowing about* is a general awareness of language structure and use. Knowing about requires a broad awareness of contexts for language use and experiences with many situations requiring variations in language use. Knowing about is developed through broad exploration and choice.

These three ways of knowing—knowing that, knowing how, and knowing about— shape the breadth and depth of knowledge from the four domains of English language arts—cognition, rhetoric, linguistics/conventions, and cultural themes or ideas from the humanities. (See Figure 1, p. xviii.)

Four Domains of Knowledge

I. *Cognition* involves two kinds of cognitive processing:

- strategies for fluent processing in basic <u>decoding</u> (refers to learning the code in reading) and <u>encoding</u> (refers to learning the code in writing);

- strategies for <u>metacognitive processing</u> (thinking about thinking), including processes for initial understanding, putting ideas together (interpretation), connecting personal experience and text, summarizing and paraphrasing, and developing a critical stance. The chart below, developed by Brian White (1995) using perspectives, strategies, and explanations from Beach and Marshall (1991), illustrates different cognitive processes at work:

Basic Perspectives	Response Strategies	Explanations of Response Strategies
Textual	Describing	"Readers describe a text when they restate or reproduce information that is provided verbatim in the text" (p. 29).
Textual	Conceiving	"When readers conceive of characters, settings, and language, they are moving beyond the description of information in order to make statements about its meaning" (p. 29).
Textual	Interpreting	"Interpreting a text involves defining the symbolic meaning, theme, or point of specific events in the text. In making interpretations, we are usually discussing what the text 'says' " (p. 143).
Textual	Close Reading	Students engaged in close reading focus on the structure of the text (rhyme scheme, meter, organization) and other aspects of the text's surface.
Social	Engaging	When readers engage a text, they "articulate their emotional reaction or level of involvement. Such responses can take a variety of forms. 'This is BORING,' 'What a dumb story,' and 'I couldn't put it down' " are typical responses (p. 28).
Social	Connecting	"It is when readers 'connect' their own experience to the materials in the text that the interactions between reader and text become most evident. The characters or situations in a story may remind us of autobiographical events or of characters and situations in other texts" (p. 31).

| Topical | Explaining | "Once we have constructed a tentative conception of characters' behavior, we must still explain as best we can why those characters are behaving as they are" (p. 30). Our explanations derive from our knowledge of social, psychological, and political forces operating on characters, and our knowledge of "topics" such as alcoholism, maturation, courtship, urban life. |
| Cultural | Judging | "When we pull away from a text . . . we make judgments about the characters in the story or about the literary quality of the text as a whole" (p. 33). Such judgments, as Scholes (1985) has argued, are based upon socially and culturally derived criteria. |

II. *Rhetoric* involves:

- <u>distance to an audience</u> (Is the audience close or detached?); and
- <u>distance to a subject</u> (Is the subject personal or impersonal? Here or there? Now or then? Is the narrator a participant or an observer?); as well as
- <u>perspective</u>: telling and showing, reliable and unreliable narrators, serious and comic, indirect (ironical) and direct.

III. *Linguistics/Conventions* (mechanics) refers to three kinds of language structures and practices:

- <u>text structures:</u> paragraphs, figures of speech, letters, literary forms, and so forth;
- <u>grammar structures:</u> phonology (sound), morphology (words), syntax (phrases and sentences);
- <u>conventions:</u> spelling, punctuation, capitalization, other editing forms. The chart below from the National Assessment of Educational Progress used the following analysis of language structure and conventions to analyze student writing (Applebee, Langer, and Mullis, 1987):

A. Sentence Types

1. Simple—A sentence that contains a subject and a verb. It may also have an object, subject complement, phrase, nominative absolute, or verbal. Also a word group used in dialogue, for emphasis, or as an exclamation that is not an independent clause.

2. Compound—A sentence containing two or more simple sentences joined by something other than a comma.

3. Complex (and compound-complex)—A sentence that contains at least one independent clause and one dependent clause.

4. Run-on

    a. Fused—A sentence containing two or more independent clauses with no punctuation or conjunction separating them.

    b. On and on—A sentence consisting of four or more independent clauses strung together with conjunctions.

    c. Comma splice—A sentence containing two or more independent clauses separated by a comma instead of a semicolon or a coordinating conjunction.

5. Fragment—A word group, other than an independent clause, written and punctuated as a sentence.

B. Faulty Sentence Construction

1. Agreement Error—A sentence in which at least one of the following occurs: subject and verb do not agree, pronoun and antecedent do not agree, noun and modifier do not agree, subject/object pronoun is misused, or verb tense shifts.

2. Awkward Sentence
   a. Faulty parallelism—A parallel construction that is semantically or structurally dysfunctional.
   b. Unclear pronoun reference—A pronoun's antecedent is unclear.
   c. Illogical construction—Faulty modification or a dangling modifier or a functionally misarranged or misproportioned sentence.
   d. Other dysfunctions—A sentence containing an omitted or extra word or a split construction that definitely detracts from readability.

C. Punctuation Errors

   Errors of commission and errors of omission in the use of commas, dashes, quotations marks, semicolons, apostrophes, and end marks.

D. Problems in Word-Level Conventions

   1. Word Choice—The writer needs a word that is different from the one written. This category also includes attempts at a verb, adjective, or adverb form that is nonexistent or unacceptable.

   2. Spelling—In addition to a misspelling, this category includes word-division errors at the end of a line, two words written as one, one word written as two, superfluous plurals, and groups of distinguishable letters that do not make a legitimate word.

   3. Capitalization—The first word in a sentence is not capitalized, a proper noun or adjective within a sentence is not capitalized, or the pronoun "I" is not capitalized.

IV. *Cultural Themes or Ideas* comprise three kinds of concepts from the humanities:

   • core concepts like the hero, history, culture, setting, and character, among others. These core concepts are part of the central narratives of English language arts;

   • dual concepts like stance (poetic and transactional), multiculturalism (difference and commonality), choice (freedom and fate), foreshadowing (ambiguity and predictability), and organization (rational and intuitive), among others;

   • metaphorical concepts that structure the narratives of English language arts (the world as a machine with part-whole relationships, life as an organism with growth over time, knowledge as a mirror or lamp, democracy as a search for common bonds).

A word needs to be said about the materials or texts focusing on the ideas of an English class. What are the ideas/themes of English? Remember that cognition, rhetoric (different audiences), and linguistics/conventions (text and conventions) are the other three domains of knowledge in English language arts, and we have grammar books, composition texts, and strategy lists to help us think about those domains. But what books and materials help us think about the ideas of English language arts? Teachers across the country attempt to answer this question when they select the literature they will purchase for a given grade level.

The books taught in nearly 5 percent or more of the seventh- and eighth-grade classrooms in the public schools are the following: *Across Five Aprils* (Hunt)*, *Animal Farm* (Orwell), *The Call of the Wild* (London)*, *The Cay* (Taylor), *A Christmas Carol* (Dickens)*, *A Day No Pigs Would Die* (Peck), *The Diary of a Young Girl* (Frank)*, *The Hobbit* (Tolkien), *The Hound of the Baskervilles* (Doyle), *Johnny Tremain* (Forbes)*, *Light in the Forest* (Richter)*, *The Miracle Worker* (Gibson), *No Promises in the Wind* (Hunt), *The Old Man and the Sea* (Hemingway), *Old Yeller* (Gibson), *The Outsiders* (Hinton)*, *The Pearl* (Steinbeck), *The Pigman* (Zindel)*, *The Prince and the Pauper* (Twain), *The Red Pony* (Steinbeck)*, *Roll of Thunder, Hear My Cry* (Taylor), *Romeo and Juliet* (Shakespeare), *Shane* (Schaefer), *Sounder* (Armstrong), *Summer of My German Soldier* (Greene), *That Was Then, This Is Now* (Hinton), *To Kill a Mockingbird* (Lee), *Tom Sawyer* (Twain)*, *Treasure Island* (Stevenson), *Where the Lilies Bloom* (Cleaver), *Where the Red Fern Grows* (Rawls)*, *The Witch of Blackbird Pond* (Speare).

*These books are in 10 percent or more of the seventh- and eighth-grade classrooms. (From Applebee, 1989).

Patterns of Development

The framework on the inside back cover shows the interaction of ways of knowing and the domains. The rubrics and commentaries are based on this framework. A given student performance—say, writing an editorial about a controversial issue—will often include all four domains and the three ways of knowing. The rubrics and commentaries will show how these domains and ways of knowing are reflected in exemplars. In addition, the rubrics and commentaries consider the developmental patterns that influence the four domains and the three ways of knowing. The domains are also shaped by the developmental patterns of the students. A developmental pattern can be influenced by a student's interests at a particular time in life or by a student's range of support and help. A student who does not receive particular kinds of help at a particular time may not achieve at a high level. An achievement level helps a teacher recognize the developmental needs of students.

The four domains of knowledge (cognition, rhetoric, linguistics/conventions, themes/ideas) are represented in the rubrics and commentaries as four kinds of developmental tensions. For example:

I. Cognition:

A. Slow Decoding/Encoding   vs.   Fluent Processing
   Fragmented   *Automatic*

Example: In development, the writer's scrawl can slowly develop into alphabetic writing.

B. No Metacognition   vs.   Metacognition: Thinking about Thinking
   Extensive scaffolding (help) by others   *Selected scaffolding (help) by others*
   Fragmented tool use   *Internal self-scaffolding and control of tools*

Example: In development, the writer or reader may begin with extensive assistance and move to more fully internalized habits of reflection on thinking.

C. Memory   vs.   Reason and Reflection
   Learning by memory only   *Learning by memory and reason/reflection*

Example: In development, the writer or reader may begin with copying and memorizing and later add interpreting and critiquing.

II. Rhetoric:

A. Reader/Writer as Audience   vs.   External Communities as Audience
   Close/personal   *Far/impersonal*

B. Reader/Writer as Subject   vs.   External World as Subject
   Close/personal   *Far/impersonal*
   Expressive subject   *Detached ("objective")*

Example: In development, the writer begins with close, personal audiences and subjects and moves toward more flexibility in writing to different audiences and on different subjects.

C. Direct Perspective   vs.   Indirect Perspective
                                     Irony/comedy

Example: In development, the writer or reader begins with a direct perspective and later adds comedy and irony.

III. Linguistics/Conventions:

A. Language/Text   vs.   Analytic Features/Paradigmatic Structures
   Synthetic/narrative case structures

Example: In development, the student begins with narrative structures and moves toward some use of analytical forms as well.

B. Small Forms   vs.   Larger Forms

Example: In development, the writer or reader begins with knowledge about small forms (sounds, letters, words) and later adds sentences and elaborated stories.

IV. Themes or Ideas:

A. Ideas/Themes   vs.
   Folk/everyday   *Scientific/academic*
   Ideas/concepts   *Concepts*
   Estimations   *Definitions*

Example: In development, the writer moves from everyday forms of knowledge to an understanding of academic forms of knowledge as well.

These are not the only developmental patterns which teachers have identified in the work of students at different ages. But these patterns illustrate some of the variations teachers attend to when they are trying to estimate growth in the English language arts. In writing and responding to literature, for example, the student is often experiencing the tensions between the personal response, which connects the text to one's internal experiences or one's values, and the analytical response, which connects the text to other texts and to ideas from the external world. The student may also be experiencing the tension between a case (for example, an autobiography) and a more generalized exposition (a larger intertextual pattern involving several cases). The student may also be trying to tell the narrative of boundary crossings, experiencing the tensions between tradition or the past and the new or present (e.g., placing Huck Finn in a contemporary problem or issue). In each instance, these tensions are part of a developmental pattern which influences the student's performance. Some of the other tensions of developmental patterns are suggested in Figure 2 on p. xix.

CONNECTIONS TO STANDARDS

The four domains of knowledge in English language arts are described in *Standards for the English Language Arts* as follows:

1. *Cognition* is described in Standards 3, 5, and 10. For example: "if [students] are reading something that is especially challenging or foreign to them, they may need to pause frequently to search for graphic, phonological, syntactic, and semantic clues that will help them make sense of the text" (page 32).

2. *Rhetoric* is described in Standards 4, 7, and 12. For example: "Even handwriting can reflect a consideration of audience: scribbles may work when writing personal notes; however, directions to others on how to get to an unknown destination will most likely require clear and complete writing" (page 34).

3. *Linguistics/conventions* are described in Standards 6, 9, and 11. For example: ". . . students need a working knowledge of the systems and structures of language as well as familiarity with accepted language conventions, including grammar, punctuation, spelling, and the formal elements of visual texts" (page 36).

4. *Themes and ideas* are described in Standards 1, 2, and 8. For example: Literary works "give students opportunities to engage in ethical and philosophical reflection on the values and beliefs of their own cultures, of other cultures, and of other times and places" (page 30).

The standards also call for all three ways of knowing—knowing that, knowing how, and knowing about. To match standards and assessments, teachers are urged to review *Standards for the English Language Arts* carefully.

Each section of this book ends with a description of how various on-demand tasks and portfolio entries represent achievement of the English standards. Because this book presents samples of students responding to challenges representing one or more of the standards for the English language arts, you can use this book to illustrate what the English standards might look like in practice. The student responses presented here are representative of high, middle, and low achievement levels within a limited sample, but these student responses are not necessarily the full range of student responses. Furthermore, many parts of the standards for the English language arts are not represented here. For example, discussion, dramatic activities, and performance on multiple-choice tests are not included. Nevertheless, the samples contained in this book should help you paint a portrait of some of your goals in the English language arts.

In the design of the book, we have made it easy to see how the exemplars and portfolios illustrate the NCTE/IRA English standards. Open up the first flap of the back cover and notice that the standards are on your right, and the samples are on your left. Of course, the list of standards included here is not a substitute for their full explanation and discussion in *Standards for the English Language Arts*, to which we refer you, but it can help you in mapping standards to exemplars. Teachers at NCTE's 1996 Spring Conference in Boston, for example, tried mapping NCTE/IRA standards to particular student performances, and those teachers found, as you will find, that the exemplars often incorporate many standards. In addition, you can use the other two books in the *Exem-*

plar Series (for grades K–5 and 9–12) to see how the exemplars for particular standards change across the grades. By looking through all three exemplar books, you will find that in general students at particular ages do better on some tasks.

If you open out the standards page, you will see a framework for assessing student performance in the English language arts. This framework is explained in detail on pages x–xv of this introduction. As you study and discuss the exemplars and portfolios, you can use the framework to generate your own descriptive statements about what a particular piece of student work shows about what a student knows and can do. The framework on the inside back flap contains some sample "starter" statements. On the innermost side of the back cover is a chart cross-referencing the on-demand exemplars and the portfolio pieces. You can use this chart to locate additional examples of particular kinds of performances (e.g., reports of information) and to identify differences and similarities between on-demand tasks and portfolio pieces. The list of various kinds of performances in on-demand tasks and portfolios appears in the table of contents.

Finally, you should use this book to start discussions with students, with fellow teachers, and with parents about achievement levels in the range and the depth of under-standing English and the English language arts. In portfolios showing several items from one student, you will find that a poor performance on one or two tasks does not necessari-ly represent what a student potentially can do, and by looking at a collection of tasks from one student, you will find out something about the student's range of skills in the English language arts. We urge you to share the student samples with your students and to ask your students to rank the samples, to write comments explaining their rankings, and then to share this information with other students. We recommend that teachers order a class set of the series in order to illustrate for students what portfolios look like and what various assignments look like. We also suggest that you ask parents to rank samples and discuss their rankings together. We recommend that you do the same with fellow teach-ers. Try scoring the student samples yourself, alone or with others, and then compare your rankings with those in the book. The rankings, the commentaries, and the rubrics come from many places across the country and have been tried out in many places, but that does not mean that your local ranking might not involve an insight into a work which the others missed. We will reserve space on NCTE's Web site for an electronic discussion of your responses (http://www.ncte.org).

REFERENCES

Applebee, A. N. (April 1989). *A study of book-length works taught in high school English courses.* Report Series 1.2. Albany: State University of New York at Albany, Center for the Learning and Teaching of Literature. ERIC #ED309453.

Applebee, A. N., Langer, J., & Mullis, I. V. S. (1987). *Grammar, punctuation, and spelling: Controlling the conventions of written English at ages 9, 13, and 17.* NAEP Report No. 15–W03. Princeton, NJ: Educational Testing Service.

Beach, R., and Marshall, J. (1991). *Teaching literature in the secondary school.* New York: Harcourt Brace Jovanovich.

Scholes, R. *Textual power: Literary theory and the teaching of English.* New Haven, CT: Yale University Press.

White, B. (1995). Assuming nothing: A pre-methods diagnostic in the teaching of literature. *English Education* 27(4), 221–239.

Figure 1 shows another way of thinking about the three types of knowledge. That is, taken together, knowing that, knowing how, and knowing about may be viewed as constituting breadth and depth in reading, writing, speaking, and listening.

Figure 1: Sample Performances for Assessing Breadth and Depth in the English Language Arts

The Three Types of Knowledge	The Four Domains of Knowledge in the English Language Arts			
	Cognition: Processing	Rhetoric: Distancing	Linguistics/Conventions: Grammar Structures, Text Structures, and Conventions	Themes/Ideas: Constructing
Reading Breadth and Depth (knowing that, knowing how, and knowing about)	Shows fluency in reading — Makes correct guesses about thoughts of characters	Depth: Reads in depth—first-person narrator — Breadth: Reads a range of narrators	Reads a range of forms—poems, novels, short stories, magazines, newspapers	Traces a single idea in history — Reads a range of opinions by different authors on same issue
Writing Breadth and Depth (knowing that, knowing how, and knowing about)	Shows automaticity in handwriting — Drafts of argument show strategies of questioning, believing, disbelieving, summarizing, clarifying — Shows evidence of editing conventions	Shows ability to shift point of view of work—from first to second person — Writes to three different audiences on public issue	Shows ability to write in different literary forms—poems, short stories—and in different nonliterary forms—reports, editorials, letters, features	Shows sense of theme, place, and character in writing of literary text
Breadth and Depth in Speaking and Listening (knowing that, knowing how, and knowing about)	Shows fluency in speaking — Drafts show use of multiple sources in development of speech	Leads small-group discussion and then reports or listens to large group in large-group discussion	Uses diverse structures in speech, from narrative to exposition and argument	Gives speech to class on public issue

These three kinds of knowledge from four different domains develop in different ways throughout the grades. Therefore, the performance of students will show some typical developmental patterns which are reflected in the samples, rubrics, and commentaries. These developmental patterns are presented in Figure 2.

Figure 2: Typical Patterns of Development in Domains of English Language Arts

The Four Domains of Knowledge in the English Language Arts

	Cognition: Processing		Rhetoric: Distancing		Linguistics/Conventions: Grammar Structures, Text Structures, and Conventions		Themes/Ideas: Constructing	
	<u>Encoding/ Decoding</u>	<u>Processing and Metacognitive Strategies</u>	<u>Distance from Audience</u>	<u>Distance from Subject</u>	<u>Text Structure</u>	<u>Grammar Modeling</u>	<u>Core Concepts</u>	<u>Dual Concepts</u>
Some Typical Developmental Patterns	From experience to mapping/drawing to print code	From recording to reporting to generalizing	From first-person experience to third-person reflections		Grammar: from sound to word to phrase		From the sense of an idea to the structure of an idea	
	From garbles and fragments to conventions and fluency From need for much assistance to selected scaffolding	From processing procedures to thinking about thinking	From expressive audience (self) to distant public audiences		Text: from narrative to paradigmatic modes Grammar: from additive to embedded structures Conventions: from letter (print) to sounds; from word (spelling) to phrase (commas)		From everyday concepts like "the hero" to scientific/academic concepts like "the psychology of leadership"	

Exemplars

This section contains exemplars of performances commonly expected of middle school students. Each exemplar consists of a description of an on-demand task, a sample of student performance, a rubric describing the achievement level of that performance, and a commentary showing the relationship of the performance to the rubric. In most cases, the exemplars appear in sets which illustrate high, middle, and low levels of performance on a common task.

At the end of each set of exemplars is a graphic ("Connections to Standards") showing which of the standards for the English language arts are illustrated by a particular performance in an on-demand setting. The second line of the graphic shows which standards might be illustrated if the performance were embedded in ongoing classroom instruction.

The majority of the exemplars in this section were selected from materials developed and published by the California Department of Education. For a number of years, the innovative assessments of writing and reading developed by California educators have provided models and inspiration for a variety of national, state, district, and school-level assessment projects. Thousands of California educators and their students participated in the development, field testing, revising, benchmarking, and scoring of the samples shown here.

The exemplars selected from California's writing and reading assessments have been slightly altered from their original format. Specifically, the rubrics which accompany the work samples have been adapted to reflect the framework presented in the introduction (pp. x–xv) of this book and on its inside back cover. Second, in the California assessments, student work received one or more numerical scores, ranging from 0 to 6. Numerical scores do not appear in this book: performances are described as being in the high, middle, or low range.

Finally, this section contains several samples of visual representation, an aspect of language use that is integrated into *Standards for the English Language Arts*. Unlike the other exemplars, these samples have not been formally ranked by teachers. They are included here with the intent of stimulating discussions about the role of visual language in assessing performance in the English language arts.

NARRATIVE (AUTOBIOGRAPHY)

Task

The first five sets of exemplars in this section are drawn from a five year assessment project originally designed by California teachers. All these student samples were completed on demand and are, therefore, first drafts. Autobiographical narrative requires writers to tell a story from their personal experience. Besides narrating an incident vividly and memorably, writers tell readers what it has meant to them. This procedure seems simple enough: writers narrate a single remembered incident and say why it was (is still) important to them. Writers focus autobiographical narratives by controlling narrative sequence and choosing relevant details. They maintain focus by centering the essay on expressing the personal importance and significance of the incident. They elaborate primarily through sensory details, remembered feelings, and specific narrative actions.

Exemplar — High

Rubric

Cognition: The writing is usually fluent. The ideas seem to flow without visible seams most of the time.

Rhetoric: There is an authentic voice that reveals to the reader the writer's attitude toward the incident. The essay includes well-chosen details, apt words, and graceful, varied sentences.

Linguistics/Conventions: The top papers are almost completely free of missteps in structure and conventions.

Themes/Ideas: The writer narrates a coherent and engaging story that moves the narrative toward the central moment. The writer locates the incident in a particular setting and orients the reader to the scene, people, and events. The essay reveals why the incident was important to the writer.

Through I remember the days events clearly, I don't recall the particular day or month in which it took place. So we'll just ~~assume~~ call it, "The day that Erik learned the truth."

Ever since I was five years old I have had a ~~dream~~ belief. I believed that if you wanted to be able to do something, I mean want with all your heart to do something, you could someday accomplish it. It may take years of practice but I believed that anything could be done, any record surpassed, and any restraint broken. I believed that folly. For you see when I was little I believed that I would grow up and make it to the big show, the grand ball, the senior prom of it all. I believed I was going to play Major League Baseball.

Now I'm not saying this is still not a dream of mine. I'm just saying I don't expect it to fall in my lap and unfold' like a fairy tale. The day I learned that I probably was not destined to rival Babe Ruth in all time greatness in the sport of baseball is still crystal clear in my mind. I played little league. baseball out was on the White Sox. Not the Chicago White Sox, just the Covina L.L. White Sox. Big difference. My season was moving along pretty well and I was batting in the clean up position, the coach thinking pretty highly of me

at the time. I started the game at short stop and got through the fielding part of the inning unscathed. The first three batters for my team got on and so I was up to bat with the bases loaded ~~Home~~ Grand slam, right? Wrong! Strike out number one. Mildly upset with myself at the time, my anger increased as I committed three errors while I was fielding grounders during the next inning. I increased my irritation by striking out again and then missing a fly ball at shortstop. The next inning found me fuming in right field after misjudging a fly ball and then committing a throwing error. My teammates (including my best friend Jason) were yelling at me to get with it, and the opposing teams fans were laughing at every blunder I made. I thought the day had gotten as bad as it could get in the last inning when I was up to bat again. I swung at the first pitch and hit a soft single up the middle. So elated was I that I threw the bat as I started to run to first base and the bat hit the umpire. The umpire proceeded to call me out even though his arm hurt so much he could hardly even make the motion. I can't describe the depression I felt as I slunk back to the bench amongst the cat-calls of the fans and groans of my teammates. I was feeling as dejected and humiliated as a child can feel.

It was after that game that I decided I probably wouldn't be able to take the kids to the baseball hall of fame and let them read about all the great games their father had played when he was in the big leagues. I decided I probably wouldn't even play in the major leagues. I was very disappointed that my belief was shattered, but at least I didn't pursue it so hard that my dream shattered me. So I decided to pursue another sport, another dream, basketball. Wouldn't a gold and yellow jersey with my last name on the back look good hanging from the rafters of the Forum?

Commentary

The writer narrates the essay, "The day that Erik learned the truth," with coherence and clarity, a strong voice, well-regulated humor, and a steady progression toward personal realization. Setting the context at a specific baseball game, the writer dramatizes the incident with specificity, using details such as "Coving L.L. White Sox," "my best friend Jason," and "yellow jersey with my name on the back." The reader hears "yelling," "laughter," and "cat-calls of the fans and groans of my teammates" and feels "dejected" and "humiliated" as the essay unfolds. Exhibiting a wonderful sense of structure, the writer discusses the wish to "grow up and make it to the big show, the grand ball, the senior prom of it all." The writer's reflection on the incident is sensitive and hopeful, and at the conclusion of the paper the writer develops a new dream as he sees his basketball jersey hanging from "the rafters of the Forum."

This writer's command of the nature of narrative plus his ability to convey the significance of this event in his life show exceptional achievement for an eighth-grade student in writing an autobiographical narrative.

Middle Exemplar

Rubric

Cognition: The writer is fluent.
Rhetoric: There is usually the voice of an earnest storyteller.
Linguistics/Conventions: The writing is clear with predictable sentences and word choice. The incident is well told but may lack some overall coherence and display limited use of strategies.
Themes/Ideas: Significance is either implied or stated.

It was christmas eve around 2am. or so.
Everyone in the house were snug in their beds ready to wake up to a cheerful Christmas day. I had been the innocent age of 7 when I learned the truth. The truth was my parents were Santa claus. As I was drifting off to dream land, my mom with the clever mind of hers wrapped a medium sized package addressed to me from Santa Claus. I was wondering about all the presents I would get in the morning.
Although I was half asleep my mind was focused on those presents under the tree. my mom figured I would be asleep, snoring or dreaming because she tiptoed into my room with the wrapped package. As she was placing the package by my side I was awakened by the rustle of paper and my mother with the most motherly look she could have given me confessed of all the years she

three batters for my team got on and so I was up to bat with the bases loaded. Grand slam, right? Wrong! Strike out number one. Mildly upset with myself at the time, my anger increased as I committed three errors while I was fielding grounders during the next inning. I increased my irration by striking out again and then missing a fly ball at shortstop. The next inning found me fuming in right field after misjudging a fly ball and then committing a throwing error. My teammates (including my best friend Jason) were yelling at me to get with it, and the opposing team's fans were laughing at every blunder I made. I thought the day had gotten as bad as it could get in the last inning when I was up to bat again. I swung at the first pitch and hit a solid single up the middle. So elated was I that I threw the bat as I started to run to first base and the bat hit the umpire. The umpire proceeded to call me out even though his arm hurt so much he could hardly even make the motion. I can't describe the depression I felt as I slunk back to the bench amongst the cat-calls of the fans and groans of my teammates. I was feeling as dejected and humiliated as a child can feel.

It was after that game that I decided I probably wouldn't be able to take the kids to the baseball hall of fame and let them read about all the great games their father had played when he was in the big leagues. I decided I probably wouldn't even play in the major leagues. I was very disapointed that my belief was shattered, but at least I didn't pursue it so hard that my dream shattered me. So I decided to pursue another sport, another dream, basketball. Wouldn't a gold and yellow jersey with my last name on the back look good hanging from the rafters of the Forum?

Commentary

The writer narrates the essay, "The day that Erik learned the truth," with coherence and clarity, a strong voice, well-regulated humor, and a steady progression toward personal realization. Setting the context at a specific baseball game, the writer dramatizes the incident with specificity, using details such as "Coving L.L. White Sox," "my best friend Jason," and "yellow jersey with my name on the back." The reader hears "yelling," "laughter," and "cat-calls of the fans and groans of my teammates" and feels "dejected" and "humiliated" as the essay unfolds. Exhibiting a wonderful sense of structure, the writer discusses the wish to "grow up and make it to the big show, the grand ball, the senior prom of it all." The writer's reflection on the incident is sensitive and hopeful, and at the conclusion of the paper the writer develops a new dream as he sees his basketball jersey hanging from "the rafters of the Forum."

This writer's command of the nature of narrative plus his ability to convey the significance of this event in his life show exceptional achievement for an eighth-grade student in writing an autobiographical narrative.

3

Exemplar

Middle

R u b r i c

Cognition: The writer is fluent.
Rhetoric: There is usually the voice of an earnest storyteller.
Linguistics/Conventions: The writing is clear with predictable sentences and word choice. The incident is well told but may lack some overall coherence and display limited use of strategies.
Themes/Ideas: Significance is either implied or stated.

It was christmas eve around 2 a.m. or so. Everyone in the house were snug in their beds ready to wake up to a cheerful christmas day. I had been the innocent age of 7 when I learned the truth. The truth was my parents were Santa claus. As I was drifting off to dream land, my mom with the clever mind of hers wrapped a medium sized package addressed to me from Santa Claus. I was wondering about all the presents I would get in the morning.

Although I was half asleep my mind was focused so those presents under the tree. My mom figured I would be asleep, snoring or dreaming because she tiptoed into my room with the wrapped package. As she was placing the package by my side I was awakened by the rustle of paper and my mother with the most motherly look she could have given me confessed of all the years she and my dad have been playing the part of Santa Claus. I was torn apart by her confession. Hadn't Santa visited the local mall? Hadn't he come to my school to pass out candy? I did not believe what my mother had told me. I just sat in bed asking myself why, shaking my head back and forth, until I fell asleep. The next morning, when I was at breakfast, every member of my family stared blankly at my expression. I said nothing for I had a feel that it was not needed. My mother, impatient with all the silence stood up and suggested that we all go and open our presents. Sure enough, as soon as she said the magic word "presents", my face brightened and beamed with light. From then on, I always thanked my parents when there was a package beside my bed addressed to me

from Santa Claus.

Exemplar — Low

Rubric

Cognition: The writer is generally fluent.

Rhetoric: The writer communicates little or no evidence of personal involvement in the incident.

Linguistics/Conventions: Lapses in sentence control or diction interfere significantly with the sense of the paper.

Themes/Ideas: The writer responds to the prompt by referring to an incident without identifying it specifically or developing it conclusively. Context may be limited or even missing. Little or no significance is implied or stated.

=Essay=

When I was little I always wanted to meet a famous baseball players. Their names are Jose Canseco, and Nolan Ryan. But as soon as I started getting older I started to think I would never see them. Because their to famous to visit any kid. They mostly visit kids that are sick, or are in a hospital. Mostly all of the famous players don't care of the kids, but there is some that care about them. I know some famous people appear at special events even though sometimes you still don't see them. Sometimes your favorite player might not even sign an autograph for their fans.

Commentary

This paper provides only minimal evidence of achievement. The writer responds only tangentially to the prompt; rather than focusing on an incident, the writer mentions a time "when I was little" and then goes on to comment about how famous players do or do not really care for kids. Although there is no actual incident related, there is a sense of an incident in the background and the feeling that, as a child, this writer was disappointed in one or more famous athletes. With direction to recall what happened one particular time when the writer tried to get an autograph, this writer could move toward a higher achievement in writing autobiographical narrative.

Connections to Standards

	STANDARDS											
On-Demand	1	2	3	4	5	6	7	8	9	10	11	12
Embedded	1	2	3	4	5	6	7	8	9	10	11	12

In an on-demand situation, an autobiographical narrative elicits performances linked primarily to writing standards 4, 5, and 6. When embedded in classroom instruction, autobiographical narrative might also require students to read and to respond to literary and nonliterary autobiographies (1, 2) and conduct research (7). Reading and responding to the autobiographies of others can help students develop an understanding of and respect for diversity (9). Students whose first language is not English might use their first language in composing autobiographical narrative (e.g., writing dialogue in or choosing to use words in the first language) (10). Students can use the autobiographical narrative genre to accomplish their own purposes, such as exploring their own life histories or creating a text for a literary magazine (11, 12).

NARRATIVE (FIRSTHAND BIOGRAPHY)

Task

Firsthand biography names a writing situation that shows how another person has been important in the writer's life. The writer shows the person through recurring activities and specific incidents that illustrate the subject's character. The writer must present this special person as memorable to readers who do not know the person, characterizing through details of appearance and manner, description of working or living environment, habits or typical activities, presentation of dialogue, or comparison to other people. In firsthand biography students explore both another person and themselves. In this type of writing, students are challenged to develop their skills in writing descriptions and narrations. Students writing a firsthand biography remember, select, and organize details and incidents that best illuminate their subjects.

Exemplar **High**

Entertainer

My dearest fat Aunt Fern steps out of her blue 1964 Buik. Chris, my brother is waiting on the porch while my mother is watering the lawn.

"Look! Auntie Fern is here! Chris spills out in joy as he sees Fern waving her arms out and yawning.

"My, my. It's so nice to be here and just inhale this fresh, Corona Air 'no smog in site!" Even though there is a stage 2 smog alert today, Aunt Fern jokes around so much that sometimes you aren't sure wheather she means what she says or not. Aunt Fern is a chubby lady, with silver hair, funny looking glasses, and has a charming face that goes along with her personality.

"Come give Fernie o hug, Christopher!" My brother hates that name and Fern knows it. Aunt Fern shrugs and says "Please don't hurt me? If you do I'll whack you with my purse!" She says laughing as Chris runs up and gives her a hug. She enters the house and sees my mom watering.

"Don't you squirt me! My finger is fat enough to plug up that hose!" My mom smiles and goes back to watering.

Paper continued on page 8

Rubric

Cognition: The student is a fluent writer.

Rhetoric: The writer can bring a subject close to the reader or move a subject to a more distant position. The writer can do the same with the persona of the narrator.

Linguistics/Conventions: The writer effectively uses a variety of sentence structures and punctuation devices. The writer often uses recurrent images to weave the descriptions together. In addition, the paper reflects careful editing, despite the few minor errors. The text structure has a clear beginning and end.

Themes/Ideas: A controlling idea, well developed and focused, dominates the paper, helping hold together the many details in the description. The absence or presence of transitions, for example, can speed up or slow down the description, having the effect of pulling the reader into the stream of events or pushing the reader back to study the pattern of events. This writer knows how to do both.

Commentary

This writer takes a risk and succeeds. The risk is in presenting the biographical subject (Aunt Fern) through a single incident, relying mainly on dialogue, and in leaving the personal significance of the relationship implicit (except for the "dearest" in the first sentence). There is much more we might have been told about Aunt Fern, but the writer, responding to the task of presenting a person whom the writer finds entertaining, nevertheless leaves us with a vivid impression of Aunt Fern as a funny, delightful, and endearing woman. The writer gives us only a few visual details; and instead of history and context about Aunt Fern, we get only the blue, sputtering 1964 Buick, a brilliantly successful detail to hold our impressions of her. In direct response to the task, the writer focuses on the humor and leaves us laughing or at least envious of Aunt Fern's humor. We do not doubt that the aunt is a memorable, significant presence in the writer's life. With time for revision and time to clean up the editing errors, this student would have an outstanding finished narrative. In any case, this is a top paper.

Aunt Fern is my Dad's sister, and they do joke around with each other quite a bit. My dad walks in the room and gives her a cup of coffie.

"Looks like you've gone on a diet! You look really skinny! My dad starts laughing and so does Auntie Fern.

"It's scale size to you brain!" We burst out in laughter. My dad sits down on the opposite couch. He rests his arm on a fuzzy pillow.

You look like a gorilla! Either that did it, Chris threw a live histeric laughing and rolling across the floor. She continued with her story about going to Africa over spring break. She made jokes about the Africans and natives, too.

Just then my dad explained that he had to pick my cousin up at a friend's house. We all came outside and my mom showed Aunt Fern our new Jeep Cherokee. He got in, started the engine, and rolled down the driveway to pick up Jason. Fern shouted out after him.

"I could do better than you without a car!" We couldn't believe how she thought of those things.

After a day at the movies my aunt left for Minnasota again. That has been the last we have seen of her, and her old 1964 Blue Buik sputtering down the street.

Entertainer

My Grandmother is the person that entertains me. She helps me make decisions about my problems. She help me see the right and wrong way to do things.

My Grandma has brown hair and hazel eyes She is five feet seven inches tall and wears dark-rimmed glasses. She has a nice figure and she wears beautiful clothes. My Grandma and I went shopping. I saw, what I though was, the most adorable kitten in the window of a well known pet store. I told her how I felt about the kitten playing quietly with the store felines. It was two day before my birthday and she wanted to give me something special. My Grandma told me that if my mom would let me care for the kitten she would buy it for me. My mom said no because we lived in an apartment. Then, my Grandma asked my mom that if she took care of it could I have it. My mom agreed to my Grandma's generous suggestion. My cat, Chappy, lived with my Grandma for four years until we bought a house.

My Grandma is extremely important to me. When I was young my mother could not support me too well. My Grandma let us stay in her enormous house. She bought me clothes, food, and all of the other things a child needs to grow up. My grandma is important to me because she helped me grow up to be the person I am today.

Rubric

Cognition: The student has control of the basic cognitive processes.

Rhetoric: The writer writes clearly enough to an audience, putting the key idea at the very beginning. But there may be a drift to other ideas which the reader may not recognize.

Linguistics/Conventions: The sentence structure is adequate, but the flow from one sentence to another is choppy. The writer has an adequate basic knowledge of conventions, but avoids risks in punctuation and spelling by using safe sentence structures.

Themes/Ideas: The writer has a controlling idea, but does not clarify the focus on that idea until the middle of the paper. By the middle of the paper, the writer introduces a central episode or compelling detail which helps hold the paper together. Some ideas appear to be repeated too often.

Commentary

Even though this student was responding to the task of writing about someone who was entertaining, he or she quickly found that his or her own focus was on how important the grandmother is. In a very solid essay, the student establishes that importance, presents the grandmother visually, and narrates one especially memorable incident. This student would benefit from frequent opportunities to write without fear of being judged; it appears that the writer's earnestness and concern with being "correct" does not allow a strong voice to come through. Nevertheless, this is a solid middle-level achievement.

Exemplar — Low

Rubric

Cognition: Many writers at the low levels are not fluent.

Rhetoric: In many low papers, about the time the main idea is beginning to emerge, the writer quits writing. Writers sometimes start social chatter with the audience and then turn away from developing the topic of the paper.

Linguistics/Conventions: The control of language structure and conventions leaves much to be desired. The overall text structure is often list-like, sometimes taking the form of one "so" after another.

Themes/Ideas: The idea of the low paper is elusive until nearly the end. The absence of a title is sometimes a clue that the writer is uncertain about the idea at the center of the paper.

I have this friend that goes to my school her name is Kim. Everyone likes her but then they don't. I think they dont like her because were ever we go there she is. I don't have a problem with her, were not best friends but were close. While we were walking down the hallway I saw that something was wrong so I asked her if she was ok she said not really so I said you can tell me she paused for a minute then said she was having problems at her house. My friends just smiled like they didnt care and that hurt me.

I had Kim call me that night so we could talk about it and we did now she seems to be a little happyer and that made me feel happyer.

Commentary

This brief essay opens with a contradictory statement about the subject, a friend of the writer. The friend, Kim, is never realized beyond naming and vague, generalized claims. One incident is referred to, but not presented. The writer does report on a dialogue but does not follow up on its possibilities. Suggestive details, nonetheless ("she paused for a minute then said," "smiled like they didnt care") hint that this writer is capable of learning strategies for writing successful firsthand biography.

Connections to Standards

	STANDARDS											
	1	2	3	4	5	6	7	8	9	10	11	12
On-Demand	1	2	3	4	5	6	7	8	9	10	11	12
Embedded	1	2	3	4	5	6	7	8	9	10	11	12

In an on-demand situation, a firsthand biography elicits performances linked primarily to the writing standards (4, 5, 6). When embedded in classroom instruction, firsthand biography might also require students to read and respond to literary and nonliterary biographies (1, 2) and conduct research (7). Reading and responding to the biographies of others can help students develop an understanding of and respect for diversity (9). Students whose first language is not English report that they use their first language in collecting data about a family narrative (e.g., interviewing a grandparent whose first language is Spanish) and in composing some firsthand biographies (e.g., writing dialogue in or choosing to use words in the first language) (10). Students can use the firsthand biography genre to accomplish their own purposes, such as exploring their family histories or contributing to a community history (11, 12).

Task

Writers must satisfy special demands when they prepare reports of information. For many students, reports of information are difficult to master. They must present themselves as authorities on a subject and impress readers with their knowledge and understanding. They must select and present enough specific details to characterize their subject for their readers. They must quickly orient readers to a subject, help keep them on track with a coherent report, and end the essay in a satisfying manner. In the best reports of information, writers express their involvement with the subject and their commitment to sharing it with readers. They develop their reports around a single theme, which they use to provide coherence to the essay. In reporting information, writers are not concerned with persuading readers to take action to correct a problem, with justifying judgments or opinions, or with presenting autobiographical disclosures. Instead, writers are concerned with informing readers about something of interest—either narratives (news reports), descriptions (profiles), or comparison-contrasts (information summaries). Reports of information may be found in textbooks, research reports, technical manuals, newspapers, letters, and essays about familiar activities and places. The key engagement with the reader is interest, which may, but does not necessarily, lead to some kind of action. Again, the original form of this task comes from California, but several other states have experimented with variations in descriptions of a favorite person, favorite book, and so forth.

Exemplar High

Neighborhood Guide

In our town there are many interesting and exciting things to do. This little town is bustling with activity from morning to night. There are hundreds of things to experience and see.

If you live near Mainstreet, there is a lovely park between Crocker Bank and Ludwig's. The park is clean, safe, and well maintained. It has a lush, green lawn that stretches the entire length of the block and is surrounded by a wall of well clipped London Plain Trees. You can go to this park and play ball, rollerskate, ride bicycles, or just stoll around the edge of the lawn.

If you prefer shopping to sports and picnics, all along Mainstreet are quaint shops and bou-

Paper continued on page 12

Rubric

Cognition: The writer is fluent and appears to use planning strategies.

Rhetoric: The writer reports the subject in an interesting and clear way, using a lively voice.

Linguistics/Conventions: The essay is well organized, and there are few errors.

Themes/Ideas: The writer includes specific information in the report —facts, details, examples, anecdotes, explanations, and definitions that are relevant to the subject and the point the writer is making. The writer states or clearly implies a controlling idea and uses it to provide coherence and a focus to the essay.

Commentary

Contributing to a neighborhood guide for the area, this student presents information about the small town of Hollister in an engaging, readable, reader-sensitive way. We never lose sight of the controlling idea, that Hollister is an interesting, attractive, bustling small town. The information is well organized and, most important, it is concrete and specific. The writer names and locates places precisely, and lists activities and options.

This essay could certainly be improved after discussion by a small group of students or a conference with the student's English teacher. For a time-limited, first draft essay, however, it exemplifies high achievement.

tiques. The shops have everything from sewing materials to candy. Things here are inexpensive and very useful. There is also a mall out toward the end of Oak St. The mall has a large, well run Macy's, a hair salon, a candy shop, a movie theater, and many other useful shops.

If you favor games and fun, there is an arcade on Mill St. The arcade has hundreds of games and prizes. It is lots of fun, and you can meet many interesting people there. If you aren't into playing arcade games, outside is miniature golf. The "golf" course consists of eighteen holes and prizes for getting "holes in one." The miniature golf course is very challenging but fun at the same time. It is supposed to be the best maintained and most difficult miniature golf course in the county.

Last but not least is the stable on River Drive. The stable is called Mr. Oak's Horse Barn by many locals. The Horse Barn has fifteen horses that you can take lessons on or rent for the day. If you take lessons, you will be instructed by a knowledgable professional in basic or advanced horse care and riding. Should you rent a horse, you have the option of taking any one of the various bridle paths that wind up into the scenic Gavillian Mountains.

I hope you can use this guide to have many adventure filled days in lovely, little Hollister.

My favorite class at Center is my English class. My teacher, Mrs. Johnson is a creative and interesting person. Everyday she tries to make up lesson plans that will make us want to learn.

To prepare us for this writing assessment Mrs. Johnson had us write stories. Then we seperated into groups. In these groups we read different papers. We then evaluated them. We also chose which paper in each pile we got was the best. We did this until there were no more papers.

Lately she has given us dittos and let us split up in pairs or threesomes and work.

The people in my class make it fun and interesting too. We have the silent-types, the loud types and we also have the kind of person who has to have his say in everything even if it has alaready been cleared up.

My class is made up of 7th an 8th graders. The only classes I have that are just 8th graders are social science and science.

English class is a place that I can just sit back and learn without having most of the problems I have with my other classes. In Englsih I can do what I like to do most, write.

A while back we had a term paper to do. It was a combined project for English and Social Science. It was fairly easy but I am glad it only comes once a year.

I guess my English class is just like yours. So I guess what I've written is the same stuff you see and do. I hope this has helped you see what a California English class is like.

Commentary

This writer, responding to the prompt to write a letter to a friend reporting on a favorite class, tells us a good deal about English class, but without any sense of the reader. The details are given in a piecemeal fashion rather than in an organized way. As is true of many writers in the middle range, an earnest tone indicates a writer willing to do what is expected. The writer likes to write. With the good teaching that seems to be going on in this English classroom, we can hope that this writer will quickly move to an understanding of how to organize a number of ideas effectively and of how to orient a report to a specific reader.

Exemplar — Low

Rubric

Cognition: The writer is somewhat fluent.

Rhetoric: The writer usually shows limited awareness of readers although he or she may reveal a lively voice.

Linguistics/Conventions: Organization may be shaky. We may not be sure of where the writer is going, though the essay will usually be readable if choppy. There are usually many serious missteps in conventions.

Themes/Ideas: Very thin development of information. Rarely will the writer use specific detail to develop a point. The essay may be no more than a simple statement of the subject.

The model T was invented by Henery Ford. Ford also invented the assembly line. The assembly line was a system that made the Model T. One person put one piece of the car together. It was much faster. In one day Henery Ford produce hundreds of Model Ts.

The Model Ts were all the same. How come they were all the same because it was cheaper. How come Henery Ford built the model T was so people can by them. Other people before Henery Ford invented the car. But they asked for too much money for them. I wouldn't know want I would do if I didn't have a car.

Commentary

Writing to sixth graders to inform them about one important invention and to report on ways the invention affects all our lives, this writer focuses on the assembly line that produced the Model T Ford. Unfortunately, the focus wavers from the assembly line to the Model T, with little information provided about either. The writer fails to report on the effect of this invention on our lives, other than to say, in the last line, "I wouldn't know want [sic] I would do if I didn't have a car." Two teachers who scored reports of information made the following observations: (1) "Many students scored lower than they might have. I think they have not been exposed to what top reports feel, look, and sound like"; (2) "The main problem I saw in the students' writing was the tendency to list facts without elaborating or explaining so that readers could understand. Students need to see examples of elaboration, and they need to learn prewriting activities for elaborating their ideas."

Connections to Standards

	STANDARDS											
	1	2	3	4	5	6	7	8	9	10	11	12
On-Demand	1	2	3	4	5	6	7	8	9	10	11	12
Embedded	1	2	3	4	5	6	7	8	9	10	11	12

In an on-demand situation, a report of information elicits performances linked primarily to writing standards 4, 5, and 6. When embedded in classroom instruction, reports of information might also require students to read and respond to a wide range of literary and nonliterary texts (1, 2) and to apply a wide range of strategies as they interpret and evaluate these texts (3). Students might also conduct research (7) and use a variety of resources to gather and synthesize information and to create and communicate knowledge (8). Depending on the topic and focus, reports of information can help students develop an understanding of and respect for diversity (9) and to use language to accomplish their own purposes (12), e.g., enjoyment or the exchange of information.

ARGUMENT (PROBLEM SOLUTION)

Task

The problem solution essay requires writers to convince specific readers of the seriousness of a problem and the feasibility of a solution (or solutions) for the problem. This requirement makes problem solution essentially argumentative or persuasive. A complex type of writing, problem solution involves several diverse writing strategies—definition, description, anecdote, causes or results, examples, or statistics—but its central strategy is argument. Writing a problem solution is a complex and challenging assignment for students. However, the assignment has the advantage of enabling students, if they decide to do so, to rely on personal experience for content. Writers maintain focus by identifying or defining a problem and asserting a solution to it. The identification and assertion provide the twin theses of problem solution essays. The writer's attitude toward the problem and solution, along with the writer's continual awareness of the readers' needs, helps the writer maintain focus. Writers organize problem solution essays by presenting the problem coherently, describing the solution clearly, and then shrewdly sequencing reasons for readers to support the solution. The prompt for this assignment asked students to propose a solution for a local problem and to address people who have the power to carry out that solution.

Exemplar High

Dear Mr. Steward,

I would like to take this opportunity to respond to the recent change of policy at the mall that prohibits teenagers under the age of sixteen from being on the premises without their parents. This rule both unfairly punishes those who do not cause problems and deprives mall merchants of a valuable source of income-the teenager's dollar.

Perhaps a more effective solution, then, is one that benefits the merchants <u>and</u> the young customers, yet is still successful in removing the problems caused by rowdy teenagers. I believe the problem could be solved by issuing all teenagers who enter the mall photo identification cards similar in appearance to a driver's license. The cards would indicate name and birthdate,

Paper continued on page 16

Rubric

Cognition: The writing shows fluency.

Rhetoric: During a paper's development, top writers often try to get people without the same views to read the evolving paper. This preplanning strategy enables writers to sharpen their understanding of the problem. The beginning of the piece engages the reader with a clearly defined problem. The writer goes directly to the problem, including some details about why it is a problem. Throughout the argument, the writer does not lose sight of the rhetorical purpose of engaging the reader. The writer often provides one or more solutions.

Linguistics/Conventions: The writer has an excellent command of language structure and the use of conventions.

Themes/Ideas: The writer shows an ability to examine a problem from more than one point of view.

Commentary

This writer is trying to convince an executive of a mall merchants' association to reconsider a rule banning students under sixteen from the mall unless they are with their parents. This writer presents a careful argument which seriously attempts to solve the problem in a way acceptable to the mall merchants. The writer controls syntax and conventions impressively; but just as important, the writer has learned how to think critically and sensitively in a complicated rhetorical situation. With every sentence, the writer reflects that he or she is thinking carefully about what might convince the merchants. The writer is tactful and strategic, but at the same time does not equivocate in the analysis of the problem, the outline of a solution, and the argument for the solution.

Although adult readers recognize that there is a likely constitutional challenge to the solution, they will concede that this thirteen-year-old writer develops an impressive argument for the rhetorical situation. For a first-draft essay, this sample is an exceptional achievement.

and underneath the personal information would be the numbers one through five. Each time an individual is found in violation of the rules of the mall, a hole would be punched through one of the numbers. Then, the date and a description would be penned in a designated area on the back of the card and the guilty party would lose mall priveleges for a previously specified amount of time.

This proposal has several advantages. The identification cards would be made quickly and easily as each teenager is admitted to the mall via a central door. Their photographs would be taken and developed by one machine, and applied to a card with personal information by another. The cost of this equipment and its operators would be far less than the price paid for damages caused by misbehavior.

A second advantage of this plan lies in the great ease with which record could be kept and entrance to the mall regulated. The information that is placed on each card issued would be stored in a computer and each time a hole is punched in a card the infraction and date would be entered into the computer as well. Thus, both the mall managers and the teenagers would know when five violations have been committed and mall priveleges lost. The computer's data would also prevent teenagers from trying to get new cards when theirs have been "filled".

Please consider my proposal, Mr. Steward. My friends and I hope to be purchasing goods at the mall again soon.

Dear Student Concil:

My name is Jeremy, a student at your school for over three years. Yesterday I saw your ad for suggestions for helping new students out with coming to a new school. I read this article with a great deal of concern. When I first came to this school I was very shy, and I was always "picked on". I had to make drastic changes to not be the "new kid", who didn't, "belong". So I slowly became more outgoing, and I didn't let other kids pick on me. Since people saw that I had guts, they admired me and became my friends. Now today, I have a great deal of friends and no problems whatsoever.

So you can see why I was very happy to see that the school wants to make it easier for the newcomers, so I wrote as soon as possible. I think I have a great solution! For each newcomer, you could assign an older person to give a very thorough and complete orientation. This way the new students would know were everything is on school grounds. There would be no wandering around or confusion. The older student would also have the responsibility of introducing the new student to some of the other students. Now to new students this is a great reishurement. This way they wouldn't get left-out or feel bad and lonely. I think these are two great solutions for a problem that could work, and it doesn't even cost anything! This way we could save the school money up for something educational! But the biggest sense of satisfaction you student concil members will know, is that new students in our school are having a great time here. This also, could promote the school so more students would come. So, please consider any offer as an alternative to making young, poor children be "hurt" by their peers.

Rubric

Cognition: The writing shows some fluency.

Rhetoric: Middle-level papers often have energy and indignation as the writer attempts to convince the reader. The writer may address the reader directly and often uses underlining and exclamation marks to convey strength of purpose. The strength of purpose is to be commended.

Linguistics/Conventions: The writer has some problems with punctuation, with spelling, and with sentence transitions. The overall text structure is loose, but not incoherent or seriously confusing.

Themes/Ideas: The idea of the argument is presented clearly, but not elaborated.

Commentary

This student writes an engaging letter to the student council, proposing a solution to the problems of new students. The writer shows a real awareness of readers and uses personal experience convincingly in the argument. Although not as strong or as polished as the high paper, this essay displays some commendable strengths. One teacher who scored this task made the following observation: "To do well with this type of writing, students need to be shown what is expected and how to accomplish it."

Exemplar — Low

Rubric

Cognition: The writing is not fluent.

Rhetoric: The writer is a little uncertain about where appeals in an argument should be addressed. Sometimes all references to the reader are missing.

Linguistics/Conventions: The paper has serious problems in conventions and language structure. It is too short to have many organizational problems at the text level.

Themes/Ideas: The writer mentions the problem but does not elaborate it. In fact, the argument seems to stop even before it gets started.

Malls

Dear Mrs. Steward,

The owner of our mall has passed a new rule saying that children under 16 can not go in the mall without a parent. This rule has caused children to leave there place that that they hang out at. some of the children are causing trouble in other places because of this rule. The mall is a public store.

I believe there is a way to satisfy both the owner and the children. One way is to hire security gards to walk around the mall. Another way is to set a certain time when thoes children may come in the mall.

Commentary

This student writes a polite, coherent letter to the president of the mall merchants' association stating the problem clearly. The writer then offers two skeletal suggestions but provides no argument for either one. The paper stops, but it does not make a gesture toward a conclusion. With guided revision opportunities, such as work in a peer-response group, this writer would undoubtedly be able to improve the effectiveness of this argument.

Connections to Standards

	STANDARDS											
	1	2	3	4	5	6	7	8	9	10	11	12
On-Demand	1	2	3	4	5	6	7	8	9	10	11	12
Embedded	1	2	3	4	5	6	7	8	9	10	11	12

In an on-demand situation, a problem solution elicits performances linked primarily to writing standards 4, 5, and 6. When embedded in classroom instruction, problem solution might also require students to read about a problem and possible solutions (1), conduct research (7), gather and synthesize information from a variey of sources (8), and create a final written product (4, 5, 6). Students can use the problem solution genre to accomplish their own purposes (12), such as influencing school policy or speaking out on issues of national concern.

Task

Evaluation, which is a form of argument, requires writers to state a judgment and support or justify that judgment with reasons and evidence. The writer of a convincing evaluation offers thoughtful, relevant reasons for the judgment and then argues them convincingly with evidence, examples, or anecdotes. A writer focuses or controls an evaluation by asserting a firm judgment and selecting relevant reasons to justify it. A writer organizes an evaluative essay through a sequence of reasons coherently developed.

Exemplar — High

Dear Tami,

I know I have been promising to write you for quite some time now, but I was so wrapped up in this spectacular book that I was reading that I forgot to write you. Down the Long Hills was definately the best book I had ever read, and I can't wait to tell you about it in person so be prepared to hear about one great book in your long awaited letter.

When you see average brothers and sisters you picture them allway fighting and yelling at each other. Well the brother and sister in this book displayed a bond of love that could never be broken. This made me realize how important your brother and sister are, and that when ever your with them you know that nobody could ever love you more than they do. The pair in this book were stranded in the wilderness and were constantly being harrased by mother nature and they never ever argued or fought among themselves. Now if that isn't a true bond than I guess I dont know what one is.

I learned a valuable lesson as I read this book. I learned that you can't give up no matter what your doing, or how hard you task is. The children in this book were confronted by snowstorms, grizzly bears and wild Indians but they never quit, they kept on going and they never gave up their search to find their papa, I truly learned a lesson in determination, and whenever I set out do something I will rember this book.

If you love heart pumping nail grinding ac-

Paper continued on page 20

Rubric

Cognition: The writer is fluent in all the basic structures.

Rhetoric: There is some confidence and authority, but the essay may be somewhat predictable or conventional. It takes time for young writers to develop the sense of authority required for a successful evaluation.

Linguistics/Conventions: There are few problems, if any, in language structures and conventions. Spelling and punctuation problems may appear, but they do not seriously damage the overall quality of the essay. The writer uses a variety of sentence structures.

Themes/Ideas: The ideas are detailed, well argued, coherent, and convincing. The writer names or identifies the subject to be evaluated and expresses a firm judgment. The writer develops at least one reason fully.

Commentary

This essay in the form of a letter recommending a favorite book to a friend represents truly commendable achievement. The writer maintains a stance toward the fictive audience with constant references to the friend, even withholding the ending of the book with a tantalizing hint. The enthusiasm of the writer points to a personal involvement in the story; the writer is quite explicit about what was learned about brother-sister relationships. More concrete evidence from the book, as further enticement, could have improved the achievement of this paper. In addition, the transition from the first to the second paragraph is awkward. Is the writer going to tell about the book in person, in the letter, or both? To keep this high score, this student will also need to improve spelling and punctuation. But the strengths of this paper overshadow the weaknesses. The writer writes with impressive conviction about his or her evaluation.

tion you'll love this book. It captures your intrest throughout the whole book. Just when you think things are slowing down the bounce back up agian and before you know it your on another hairraising adventure. I would say being chased by bandits, hunted by wolves, shot at by Indians could satisfy anyones need for action.

Its to bad that I cant tell you how it ends but I guess youll just have to wait and find out for youself. I know this letter is long overdue but I certainly believe that writing to you about this book has made up for how late it is

Exemplar **Middle**

Rubric

Cognition: The writer is fluent.

Rhetoric: The writer demonstrates the ability to develop an argument justifying an evaluation, but lacks confidence. The writer may express authority, but does so without the fresh thinking revealed in apt word choices and variations in sentences.

Linguistics/Conventions: The paper may lack sentence variety, but the basics of structure and conventions are adequate.

Themes/Ideas: The writer identifies the subject to be evaluated and expresses a firm judgment of it. The essay includes at least one reason that is moderately developed but the reason may not be developed in a sustained, convincing way.

Dear Joe,
I am sending this book, <u>Across five Aprils</u>, for you to read it, I found this book about a boy's life during the Civil War very enjoyable, especially once I got into the different levels of it. I think you would like the danger and the irony in this book the most.

One part that is full of excitement and danger and is ironic is when Dave Burdow, the low life, saves Jethro, the main character, form certain doom. If Dave had not taken the reins of the horses Guy, Wortman, the local bully and thief, would of caused the wagon to fall off a bridge killing Jethro. Another part that is good is when Jethro thinks fighting was great and then he changes mind after one of his brothers get killed in the war.

Well, I don't want to spoil the book for you, so I will stop telling you about it. Read this book next week. By the way, I will want to hear how you like this book. I'm sure you won't be sorry.

Commentary

This evaluation of a favorite book takes the same letter form that the previous essay did, but the contrast is significant. In this middle essay, the student frames the essay with an awareness of "Joe," a real or fictive friend; but the central part of the essay, containing the reasons and evidence, is lifeless, voiceless — a flat sequence of the parts of the book that were "good." While the specific anecdotes from the book are well chosen, they are not adequately developed or contextualized.

My favorite music is rock. It has alot of beat into it. It also has many more new technology instruments. Most of it is electric. Like guitars, drums, and keybords. All of this equipment is more louder. I think it sounds alot better. Everything in this music is just perfect. In the way they make it. This music has made me like rock music. I think it is good. It really gets you going and feeling good.

Rubric

Cognition: The writer may be fluent in the code but not fluent in the flow of sentences. The writer may appear to be thinking one sentence at a time.

Rhetoric: Voice and style are often flat and perfunctory.

Linguistics/Conventions: Low papers are often either full of errors and inventive energy or flat and nearly error-free.

Themes/Ideas: The writer states a judgment but may not give any reasons to support the judgment. Instead, the writer describes or summarizes the subject being evaluated or may list reasons (some of which may not be relevant).

Commentary

In this essay, the judgment is stated, but the reasons supporting the judgment—the beat, "new technology instruments," and "feeling good"—are not elaborated. The essay seems to be a random sequence of statements about the writer's favorite music. One teacher made the following observations about scoring these types of arguments: "I think good evaluative writing is difficult even for good students. As I see it, most kids have trouble doing more than just summarizing. They need to learn to develop substantial reasoning behind why they like or dislike something."

Connections to Standards

	STANDARDS											
	1	2	3	4	5	6	7	8	9	10	11	12
On-Demand	1	2	3	4	5	6	7	8	9	10	11	12
Embedded	1	2	3	4	5	6	7	8	9	10	11	12

In an on-demand situation, an evaluation elicits performances linked primarily to writing standards 4, 5, and 6. When embedded in classroom instruction, evaluation might also require students to read and respond to a wide range of literary and nonliterary texts (1, 2) and to apply a wide range of strategies as they interpret and evaluate these texts (3). Students might conduct research (7) and use a variety of resources to gather and synthesize information to create and communicate knowledge (8) about the object of evaluation. Depending on their topics and focus, evaluation tasks can help students develop an understanding of and respect for diversity (9) and to use language to accomplish their own purposes (12), such as reviewing a concert for a local newspaper or selecting a stereo system.

RESPONSE TO LITERATURE (ANALYSIS)

Task

The responses used in this section were gathered from the 1992 survey of America's students by the National Assessment of Educational Progress (NAEP), *Reading Assessment Redesigned: Authentic Texts and Innovative Instruments in NAEP's 1992 Survey*. The 1992 assessment required students to reflect on and write about their understandings of one or more literary selections.

This task has two types of constructed response. The *first type* of constructed-response question is short, asking students to think and write briefly about their understandings. The *second type* (question 4) is an extended constructed-response question and is designed to prompt greater thought and reflection. In comparison to the multiple-choice questions that required students to select among an array of already developed responses, both types of constructed-response questions required students to generate their own ideas and to communicate them in writing.

In this assessment students read and responded to two texts. "Cady's Life" is a story written by Anne Frank when she was hiding in an attic to escape persecution by Hitler and the Nazis during World War II. It is told in the first person by a Christian girl named Cady and is about her experiences with and sorrow for her friend Mary, who is Jewish and who is eventually arrested along with the rest of her family. The story was preceded with brief biographical information about Anne Frank. Students were expected to use this information in some of their responses. Also, the story was paired with a poem, "I Am One," by Edward Everett Hale, in which Hale acknowledges that one person can always do something: "I will not refuse to do the something that I can do."

The following rubric/framework was used to evaluate the reading responses. The rubric for literary responses focuses on accomplishment in initial understanding, development of an interpretation, personal reflection, and critical stance. Responses to the short constructed-response questions (questions 1–3) were scored as either acceptable or unacceptable. Responses to the extended question (question 4) were scored according to a four-point scale as extensive, essential, partial, or unsatisfactory. Three levels of response–high, middle, low–are presented here. Another type of NAEP rubric is shown on page 32. The levels show degrees of accomplishment in various aspects of reading literacy as outlined in the rubric/framework:

NAEP's 1992 READING RUBRIC/FRAMEWORK
Constructing, Extending, and Examining Meaning

	Initial Understanding	Developing an Interpretation	Personal Reflection and Response	Demonstrating a Critical Stance
	Requires the reader to provide an initial impression or unreflected understanding of what was read.	Requires the reader to go beyond the initial impression to develop a more complete understanding of what was read.	Requires the reader to connect knowledge from the text with personal background knowledge. The focus here is on how the text relates to personal knowledge.	Requires the reader to stand apart from the text and consider it.
Reading for Literary Experience	What is the story/plot about?	How did the plot develop?	How did this character change your idea of _____?	Rewrite this story with ___ as a setting or ___ as a character.
	How would you describe the main character?	How did this character change from the beginning to the end of the story?	Is this story similar to or different from your own experiences?	How does this author's use of ___ (irony, personification, humor) contribute to ___?
Reading for Information	What does this article tell you about _____?	What caused this event?	What current event does this remind you of?	How useful would this article be for _____? Explain.
	What does the author think about this topic?	In what ways are these ideas important to the topic or theme?	Does this description fit what you know about _____? Why or why not?	What could be added to improve the author's argument?
Reading to Perform a Task	What is this supposed to help you do?	What will be the result of this step in the directions?	In order to ___, what information would you need to find that you don't know right now?	Why is this information needed?
	What time can you get a nonstop flight to X?	What must you do before this step?	Describe a situation in which you could leave out step X.	What would happen if you omitted this?

QUESTION 1: Why did the author write this story from the perspective of Cady, a Christian?

Some short constructed-response questions were designed to determine whether students could demonstrate a critical stance. For example, the question above asked students in the eighth grade to employ their critical powers to think about the point of view taken in the short story written by Anne Frank, "Cady's Life." No middle score was given on questions 1–3.

Commentary

Acceptable responses like this one indicated an understanding of what a reader could learn from Cady's perspective, and the utility of Cady's perspective for Frank. These responses often focused on how Frank wanted to explore what Christians felt about the fate of the Jews.

Asking readers to consider why the author presents information from a particular perspective requires the ability to take a critical stance toward the passage. That is, readers must step back from their text-based understanding, think objectively about how the author has crafted the piece, and make evaluative decisions about why the author may have done so.

> She was able to see things from the outside. She never really knew what they did to the Jews but yet still felt pain in losing her friend. She represented the thoughts & feelings of the germans against the occupation.

Commentary

Unacceptable responses to this question either did not focus on perspective at all, or showed confusion about why the author might have been interested in using Cady's feelings to frame the story. Such responses indicated a difficulty in grasping how a particular perspective might function in a text.

> The author wrote this story from the perspective of Cady, a Christian because she was also with her and her family, she knows what happened.

QUESTION 2: Read the poem "I Am One." For Anne Frank, what was "the something that I can do?"

Another important reading skill is developing an interpretation by using one text, possibly of a different genre, to better understand another. The question above required students to use their understanding of the poem "I Am One," by Edward Everett Hale to think about the biographical information provided at the beginning of "Cady's Life."

> I Am One
> I am only one,
> But still I am one.
> I cannot do everything,
> But still I can do something;
> And because I cannot do everything
> I will not refuse to do the something that I can do.

Exemplar — High

Commentary

Acceptable responses showed an understanding of the different kinds of information in the story and in the biographical piece; students who wrote these responses were able to distinguish between Frank as a writer and the characters Frank created, and thus to think about Frank's life in the abstract, and to consider the meaning of the creation of "Cady's Life" in the context of the poem. Many of the responses discussed Anne Frank's decision to write about her experiences.

> She could write down what it was like on others would know what cruelty the German's preformed She gave the word Jewish a face so others realized it was not just a Jew that was killed it was a person with hopes & fears like the rest of us,

Exemplar — Low

Commentary

Unacceptable responses indicated a lack of understanding of the texts themselves and of how to use different texts or genres to develop an interpretation. They were characterized by vague statements about what Anne Frank may have been feeling that indicated a weak grasp of her circumstances. Other responses offered an interpretation of the poem without any real attempt to use the poem to consider Frank's life.

> Anne felt helpless because she couldn't do anything.

QUESTION 3: Explain what the author means when she says that slamming doors symbolized the closing of the door of life.

The above question required students to develop an interpretation by thinking critically about the text of "Cady's Life." This question attempted to sample students' ability to understand figurative language, an important reading skill. Responses to this question did not have a middle score.

Exemplar High

Commentary

Acceptable responses showed an overall understanding of the text and an understanding of the symbol of the slamming doors. Acceptable responses like the one shown here focused on how the slamming doors meant that people were being taken away and probably killed, or prevented from returning to their ways of life.

> The slamming door symbolizes the nazi's shutting out the Jews and later shutting them out of existence their door to life had been slammed.

Exemplar Low

Commentary

Unacceptable responses demonstrated an inability to interpret the text and to explain the author's meaning. They were often vague, either restating the question or presenting thoughts about the text without explanation.

> She means that when you close a door its like closing the door of life.

QUESTION 4: How does the poem "I Am One" help you to understand Anne Frank's life? Use information from the introduction to the story to explain your ideas.

This extended question, posed to eighth graders who read Anne Frank's short story "Cady's Life," is an intertextual task. It asked students to explore the relationships between the poem and Frank's own life, as elaborated in the brief biographical introduction to her story. (Responses to this question were scored according to a four-point scale: extensive, essential, partial, or unsatisfactory. Three levels are presented here.)

Exemplar **High**

Commentary

To respond to this question beyond a cursory level, students needed to understand both the poem and the information about Anne Frank's life , and they needed to perceive connections between the poem and Anne's life. Sudents needed to identify one issue in both the poem and Anne's life.

Extensive understanding was reflected in high responses, which used the relationship between the poem and Anne Frank's life to discuss the larger significance of her life, such as how she preserved history through her writing.

In the poem Hule is talking about how an individual can even make a difference in the world. Anne Frank made a big difference in the world when it came to understanding different people. Her diary and writing have proved and inspiration to those around this world. She has influenced people to realize what a stupid thing moral intolerance is, and maybe there will never be another Holocaust because of her writing.

Exemplar **Middle**

Commentary

Middle papers showed partial understanding. They provided some evidence that the student understood the relationship between the poem and Anne Frank's life, but these responses usually described the relationship without concrete explanation or relevant examples.

It helps by saying who Anne Frank is. It also helps by telling what Anne can do. It helps by telling that one person can make a difference.

Exemplar — Low

> Her life was very sad. She lived during World War II. So she heard alot of noises during the night. I know exactly the way she feels.

Commentary

Low papers exhibited little or no understanding of the poem or of Anne Frank's life, or did not posit a relationship between the two texts. Often these papers focused on trivial or tangential issues.

The National Assessment of Educational Progress also used for some assessments the following condensed rubric:

Level 4	**Elaborated** Students providing elaborated responses went beyond the essential, reflecting a higher level of coherence and providing more detail to support the points made.
Level 3	**Adequate** Students providing adequate responses included the information and ideas necessary to accomplish the underlying task and were considered likely to be effective in achieving the desired purpose.
Level 2	**Minimal** Students writing at the minimal level recognized some or all of the elements needed to complete the task but did not manage these elements well enough to assure that the purpose of the task would be achieved.
Level 1	**Unsatisfactory** Students who wrote papers judged as unsatisfactory provided very abbreviated, circular, or disjointed responses that did not even begin to address the writing task.
Level 0	**Not Rated** A small percentage of the responses were blank, indecipherable, completely off task, or contained a statement to the effect that the student did not know how to do the task; these responses were not rated.

(From NAEP, Trends in Academic Progress by Ina V. S. Mullis, John A. Dossey, Mary Foerth, Lee R. Jones, and Claudia Gentile, 1991. Educational Testing Service, p. 147.)

Connections to Standards

	STANDARDS											
On-Demand	1	2	3	4	5	6	7	8	9	10	11	12
Embedded	1	2	3	4	5	6	7	8	9	10	11	12

In an on-demand situation, response to literary and informational texts requires students to apply a range of strategies to comprehend, interpret, evaluate, and critique texts (1, 2, 3, 6). When embedded in classroom instruction, responses might include visual representations (4) and texts might also include such nonprint sources as films and television and radio broadcasts (1). Depending on the texts being read or viewed and the responses being elicited or offered, responses to literary and informational texts can help students develop an understanding of and respect for diversity (9). The materials above certainly do that. Students whose first language is not English can use their first language to develop understanding of texts (e.g., recording marginal notes, noting questions, translating key concepts into the first language) (10). Students can use responses to literary and informational texts to accomplish their own purposes, such as developing and exploring an interpretation of a self-selected novel or becoming informed on a political issue (12).

Response to Literature

Task

The following reading task, taken from "A Sampler of English-Language Arts Assessment—Middle Grades" from the California Department of Education, asks students to read a selection about the life of Albert Einstein written by his friend, Banesh Hoffmann. The student's score is determined by evaluating all the evidence of the performance, whether in the form of marginal notes, graphics, or extended written responses. The first step in this response was to write marginal comments while reading. Responses from Student A are on the left and Student B on the right. How would you judge these comments?

Before You Read: You are going to read a selection about the life of Albert Einstein written by his friend. Before you read, take a minute to think of what you already know about Einstein.

As you read, you may mark up the selection in any way that helps you better understand or remember what you are reading.

My thoughts, feelings, and/or questions about what I'm reading*

*In the test for 1994, this wording has been changed to: My thoughts and/or questions about what I'm reading.

Student A

How could simplicity result in Einstein's success?

Why would Einstein want a salary that was so small?

Einstein was friendly and at ease w/ himself.

Einstein was very modest.

I wonder if being such a prodigy had an effect on Einstein's late learning ability.

My Friend, Albert Einstein

by Banesh Hoffmann

He was one of the greatest scientists the world has ever known, yet if I had to convey the essence of Albert Einstein in a single word, I would choose *simplicity*. Perhaps an anecdote will help. Once, caught in a downpour, he took off his hat and held it under his coat. Asked why, he explained, with admirable logic, that the rain would damage the hat, but his hair would be none the worse for its wetting. This knack of going instinctively to the heart of a matter was the secret of his major scientific discoveries—this and his extraordinary feeling for beauty.

I first met Albert Einstein in 1935, at the famous Institute for Advanced Study in Princeton, N.J. He had been among the first to be invited to the Institute, and was offered *carte blanche* as to salary. To the director's dismay, Einstein asked for an impossible sum: it was far too *small*. The director had to plead with him to accept a larger salary.

I was in awe of Einstein, and hesitated before approaching him about some ideas I had been working on. When I finally knocked on his door, a gentle voice said, "Come"—with a rising inflection that made the single word both a welcome and a question. I entered his office and found him seated at a table, calculating and smoking his pipe. Dressed in ill-fitting clothes, his hair characteristically awry, he smiled a warm welcome. His utter naturalness at once set me at ease.

As I began to explain my ideas, he asked me to write the equations on the blackboard so he could see how they developed. Then came the staggering—and altogether endearing—request: "Please go slowly. I do not understand things quickly." This from Einstein! He said it gently, and I laughed. From then on, all vestiges of fear were gone.

Einstein was born in 1879 in the German city of Ulm. He had been no infant prodigy; indeed, he was so late in learning to speak that his parents feared he was a dullard. In school, though his teachers saw no special talent in him, the signs were already there. He taught himself calculus, for example, and his teachers seemed a little afraid of him because he asked questions they could not answer. At the age of 16, he asked himself whether a light wave would seem stationary if one ran

My thoughts, feelings, and/or questions about what I'm reading*

*In the test for 1994, this wording has been changed to: My thoughts and/or questions about what I'm reading.

Student B

He took care of his things. He didn't care about what happen to his hair

didn't care about money.

He was not very smart at a young age

Student A

How could someone who taught himself calculus fail an entrance exam?

Einstein was amazing enough to link 2 controversial theories together in order to equate to something that was true.

Einstein was a professional.

Did Einstein have a fear of not knowing something.

Einstein thought with ease and seemed relaxed,

How did Einstein eventually find the will-power to form more theories even after his wife died.

He was scientifically religious.

---

abreast of it. From that innocent question would arise, ten years later, his theory of relativity.

Einstein failed his entrance examinations at the Swiss Federal Polytechnic School in Zurich, but was admitted a year later. There he went beyond his regular work to study the masterworks of physics on his own. Rejected when he applied for academic positions, he ultimately found work in 1902 as a patent examiner in Berne, and there in 1905 his genius burst into fabulous flower.

Among the extraordinary things he produced in that memorable year were his theory of relativity, with its famous offshoot, $E = mc^2$ (energy equals mass times the speed of light squared), and his quantum theory of light. These two theories were not only revolutionary, but seemingly contradictory: the former was intimately linked to the theory that light consists of waves, while the latter said it consists somehow of particles. Yet this unknown young man boldly proposed both at once—and he was right in both cases, though how he could have been is far too complex a story to tell here.

Collaborating with Einstein was an unforgettable experience. In 1937, the Polish physicist Leopold Infeld and I asked if we could work with him. He was pleased with the proposal, since he had an idea about gravitation waiting to be worked out in detail. Thus we got to know not merely the man and the friend, but also the professional.

The intensity and depth of his concentration were fantastic. When battling a recalcitrant problem, he worried it as an animal worries its prey. Often, when we found ourselves up against a seemingly insuperable difficulty, he would stand up, put his pipe on the table, and say in his quaint English, "I will a little tink" (he could not pronounce the "th"). Then he would pace up and down, twirling a lock of his long graying hair around his forefinger.

A dreamy, faraway and yet inward look would come over his face. There was no appearance of concentration, no furrowing of the brow—only a placid inner communion. The minutes would pass, and then suddenly Einstein would stop pacing as his face relaxed into a gentle smile. He had found the solution to the problem. Sometimes it was so simple that Infeld and I could have kicked ourselves for not having thought of it. But the magic had been performed invisibly in the depths of Einstein's mind, by a process we could not fathom.

When his wife died he was deeply shaken, but insisted that now more than ever was the time to be working hard. I remember going to his house to work with him during that sad time. His face was haggard and grief-lined, but he put forth a great effort to concentrate. To help him, I steered the discussion away from routine matters into more difficult theoretical problems, and Einstein gradually became absorbed in the discussion. We kept at it for some two hours, and at the end his eyes were no longer sad. As I left, he thanked me with moving sincerity. "It was fun," he said. He had had a moment of surcease from grief, and then groping words expressed a deep emotion.

Although Einstein felt no need for religious ritual and belonged to no formal religious group, he was the most deeply religious man I have known. He once said to me, "Ideas come from God," and one could hear the

---

Student B

His theory was known forever $E = mc^2$

He worried about failing. But if it did he would try again

He would think until he got the answer to a problem.

After his wifes death he was sad but didn't stop working he pushed hisselfe harder.

He had no religio but believed in god.
He had a saying that meant scie could have difficu doing something t not hopeless.

My thoughts, feelings, and/or questions about what I'm reading

Student A

What's the difference between composing and creating.

Did Einstein used everyday, normal simulations in order to create theories?

Sometimes the most obvious is the least obvious.

What is the speaker trying to relate with Einstein and time?

It's funny how his friend realized Einstein's fame but Einstein was unaware of it when it walked up to him.

---

capital "G" in the reverence with which he pronounced the word. On the marble fireplace in the mathematics building at Princeton University is carved, in the original German, what one might call his scientific credo: "God is subtle, but he is not malicious." By this Einstein meant that scientists could expect to find their task difficult, but not hopeless: the Universe was a Universe of law, and God was not confusing us with deliberate paradoxes and contradictions.

Einstein was an accomplished amateur musician. We used to play duets, he on the violin, I at the piano. One day he surprised me by saying Mozart was the greatest composer of all. Beethoven "created" his music, but the music of Mozart was of such purity and beauty one felt he had merely "found" it—that it had always existed as part of the inner beauty of the Universe, waiting to be revealed.

It was this very Mozartean simplicity that most characterized Einstein's methods. His 1905 theory of relativity, for example, was built on just two simple assumptions. One is the so-called principle of relativity, which means, roughly speaking, that we cannot tell whether we are at rest or moving smoothly. The other assumption is that the speed of light is the same no matter what the speed of the object that produces it. You can see how reasonable this is if you think of agitating a stick in a lake to create waves. Whether you wiggle the stick from a stationary pier, or from a rushing speedboat, the waves, once generated, are on their own, and their speed has nothing to do with that of the stick.

Each of these assumptions, by itself, was so plausible as to seem primitively obvious. But together they were in such violent conflict that a lesser man would have dropped one or the other and fled in panic. Einstein daringly kept both—and by so doing he revolutionized physics. For he demonstrated they could, after all, exist peacefully side by side, provided we gave up cherished beliefs about the nature of time.

Science is like a house of cards, with concepts like time and space at the lowest level. Tampering with time brought most of the house tumbling down, and it was this that made Einstein's work so important—and controversial. At a conference in Princeton in honor of his 70th birthday, one of the speakers, a Nobel Prize winner, tried to convey the magical quality of Einstein's achievement. Words failed him, and with a shrug of helplessness he pointed to his wristwatch, and said in tones of awed amazement, "It all came from this." His very ineloquence made this the most eloquent tribute I have heard to Einstein's genius.

Although fame had little effect on Einstein as a person, he could not escape it; he was, of course, instantly recognizable. One autumn Saturday, I was walking with him in Princeton discussing some technical matters. Parents and alumni were streaming excitedly toward the stadium, their minds on the coming football game. As they approached us, they paused in sudden recognition, and a momentary air of solemnity came over them as if they had been reminded of a different world. Yet Einstein seemed totally unaware of this effect and went on with the discussion as though they were not there. We think of Einstein as one concerned only with the deepest aspects of science. But he saw scientific principles in everyday things to which most of us would give barely a second thought. He once asked me if I had ever

---

My thoughts, feelings, and/or questions about what I'm reading

Student B

He was a musician (violin).

Einstein was always glad that he finished his work and thank the time for giving him the life todo

Einstein did not care if he was famous or not.

He didn't think he was so great that people admired him.

How does he come up with great answers

Student A marginal notes:

The sand and surface tension is such an awesome example! I always wondered about the raindrops on a windowpane.

Einstein's little thoughts created one big puzzle.

Einstein's theories were controversial yet amazing.

What is it meant to put a price on your head?

Why did Einstein sign the letter in the first place? Wasn't he aware that something like this would have happened?

What?! He didn't give them any money?!

That's sad that Einstein died before his friend. What is it meant by "the revelation of great art that lets one see what was formerly hidden"?

Great story, I wonder if it was all true.

Center printed text:

wondered why a man's feet will sink into either dry or completely submerged sand, while sand that is merely damp provides a firm surface. When I could not answer, he offered a simple explanation.

It depends, he pointed out, on *surface tension*, the elastic-skin effect of a liquid surface. This is what holds a drop together, or causes two small raindrops on a windowpane to pull into one big drop the moment their surfaces touch.

When sand is damp, Einstein explained, there are tiny amounts of water between grains. The surface tensions of these tiny amounts of water pull all the grains together, and friction then makes them hard to budge. When the sand is dry, there is obviously no water between grains. If the sand is fully immersed, there is water between grains, but no water *surface* to pull them together.

This is not as important as relativity; yet there is no telling what seeming trifle will lead an Einstein to a major discovery. And the puzzle of the sand does give us an inkling of the power and elegance of his mind.

Einstein's work, performed quietly with pencil and paper, seemed remote from the turmoil of everyday life, but his ideas were so revolutionary they caused violent controversy and irrational anger. Indeed, in order to be able to award him a belated Nobel Prize, the selection committee had to avoid mentioning relativity, and pretend the prize was awarded primarily for his work on the quantum theory.

Political events upset the serenity of his life even more. When the Nazis came to power in Germany, his theories were officially declared false because they had been formulated by a Jew. His property was confiscated, and it is said a price was put on his head.

When scientists in the United States, fearful that the Nazis might develop an atomic bomb, sought to alert American authorities to the danger, they were scarcely heeded. In desperation, they drafted a letter which Einstein signed and sent directly to President Roosevelt.

It was this act that led to the fateful decision to go all-out on the production of an atomic bomb—an endeavor in which Einstein took no active part. When he heard of the agony and destruction that his $E = mc^2$ had wrought, he was dismayed beyond measure, and from then on there was a look of ineffable sadness in his eyes.

There was something elusively whimsical about Einstein. It is illustrated by my favorite anecdote about him. In his first year in Princeton, on Christmas Eve, so the story goes, some children sang carols outside his house. Having finished, they knocked on the door and explained they were collecting money to buy Christmas presents. Einstein listened, then said, "Wait a moment." He put on his scarf and overcoat, and took his violin from its case. Then, joining the children as they went from door to door, he accompanied their singing of "Silent Night" on his violin.

How shall I sum up what it meant to have known Einstein and his works? Like the Nobel Prize winner who pointed helplessly at his watch, I can find no adequate words. It was akin to the revelation of great art that lets one see what was formerly hidden. And when, for example, I walk on the sand of a lonely beach, I am reminded of his ceaseless search for cosmic simplicity—and the scene takes on a deeper, sadder beauty.

Student B marginal notes:

They did not want to give him credit for the relativity theory but won a noble prize for the quantum theor. the Nazis wanted to prove him wrong

He felt as if all his problem answers were wrong cause of them. But didn't give He went to princeton

Note: Student A is the high score and Student B is the middle score. Student C (the low score) did not make marginal notes.

The outstanding (high) responses of Student A were judged using the following rubric, which includes the four domains of knowledge. The score was based on the marginal notes that appear in the lefthand column that runs alongside the story, as well as the responses to questions 1–7, which follow. A summary commentary appears at the end of Student A's responses.

R u b r i c

Cognition: The best readers are fluent readers, able to process print with ease. These good readers take risks. They entertain challenging ideas and explore multiple possibilities of meaning as they read, grounding these meanings in their acute perceptions of textual and cultural complexities. They often revise their understanding of a text as they reread and as additional information or insight becomes available to them. They fill in gaps in a text, making warranted and responsible assumptions about unstated causes or motivations, or drawing meaning from subtle cues. They are able to change their minds, to articulate a newly developed level of understanding.

Rhetoric: Top readers challenge the text. They carry on a dialogue with the writer, raising questions, taking exception, agreeing or disagreeing, appreciating or criticizing text features. They may sometimes suggest ways of rewriting the text. They may test the validity of the author's ideas or information by considering the authority of the author and the nature and quality of evidence presented. They may speculate about the ideology or cultural or historical biases that seem to inform a text, sometimes recognizing and embracing and sometimes resisting the position that a text seems to construct for its reader.

Linguistics/Conventions: An exemplary reading performance is insightful, discerning, and perceptive as the reader constructs and reflects on structures in a text. Readers at this level are sensitive to linguistic, cultural, and psychological nuances and complexities. They differentiate between literal and figurative meanings.

Themes/Ideas: Readers develop connections with and among texts. They recognize real or seeming contradictions, exploring possibilities for their resolution or tolerating ambiguities. They demonstrate their understanding of the whole work as well as an awareness of how the parts work together to create the whole. They connect their understanding of the text not only to their own ideas, experience, and knowledge, but to their history as participants in a culture or larger community, often making connections to other texts or other works of art. Exceptional readers draw on evidence from the text to generate, validate, expand, and reflect on their own ideas.

---

1. What are your thoughts and feelings about what you have read? Take a few minutes to write your ideas.*

*In the test for 1994, this wording has been changed to:
What is your first response to the story? Take a few minutes to write your ideas, questions, or opinions about this story.

Originally, I thought of Einstein as a prestigious and notable person that thought of basically impossible, but true, theories. After having read this; I discovered that Einstein was much more than a scientist and mathematician. He was a person who educated himself with music and the art of nature. Einstein didn't care that something worked, he cared how and why something worked and what place it held within the universe. Einstein's life was much like the life of anyone else. He was directly effected in what happened in the world or with his own life. All Einstein really cared about was living life. He didn't seem like the person who did the things he did just to receive fame and fortune. To my generation, Einstein would never seem a simplictic man, his theories and numbers are all too original and confusing. However, he was a simple man, he lived life by fulfilling the necessities of food and shelter and by conversing with the world and nature.

Student A

High

2. Think about Einstein as a person and a scientist. In the split "profile" and below, use symbols, images, drawings, and/or words to give your ideas about Einstein the person and Einstein the scientist.

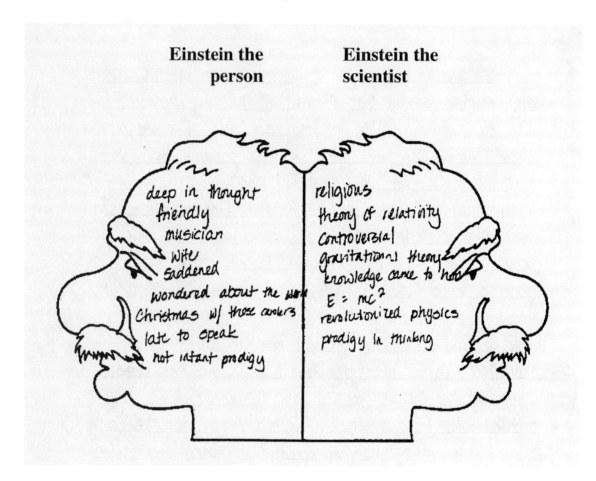

Einstein the person

deep in thought
friendly
musician
wife
saddened
wondered about the world
Christmas w/ those carolers
late to speak
not infant prodigy

Einstein the scientist

religious
theory of relativity
controversial
gravitational theory
knowledge came to him
$E = mc^2$
revolutionized physics
prodigy in thinking

3. Explain how the symbols, images, drawings, and/or words in your "profiles" represent your ideas about Einstein.

as a person:

Einstein was a friendly man who was effected by the things that happened to him. He was easily saddened after they used his theory to build on atomic bombs and by his wife dying. Einstein probably did more thinking as a regular person instead of some infant prodigy that had a lot of knowledge. He wondered about the world in order to achieve so much knowledge. Even though he was late to speak, he indulged himself by putting together puzzle pieces of nature.

as a scientist:

Even though Einstein had no formal religion, he received his knowledge from religion. His religious-scientific ideals about thinking got him to come up with the theory of relativity, gravitational theory, and $E = mc^2$. Einstein's scientific ideals that got him to become so controversial was because of simplicity. His simplicity in thinking and reasoning made him a prodigy, a mix of knowledge and common sense.

Student A   High

4. Think about Einstein the scientist and Einstein the person. Choose an example from the reading selection that shows how Einstein's personal characteristics affected him as a scientist.

Einstein's personal characteristics affected him as a scientist. One example of this was when Einstein signed the letter from the scientists who were afraid the Nazis were building an atomic bomb. Because of this, U.S. also decided to build an

Einstein's personal characteristics affected him as a scientist. One example of this was when Einstein signed the letter from the scientists who were afraid the Nazis were building an atomic bomb. Because of this, U.S. also decided to build an atomic bomb, a total disregard for the value and respect of life. After this incident, Einstein always had a look of sadness and remorse in his eyes even though he took no part in it. Einstein's scientific theory was the key in building the bomb. However, as much as any other scientist would praise himself for being so brilliant, Einstein punished himself by feeling responsible for those who died. Einstein's personal beliefs had a strong effect on how he applied his scientific concepts. Einstein had too much respect and appreciation for the balance of nature, the world, and life in order to be responsible for the atomic bomb.

5. Based on your reading, if you were going to talk to Einstein, what would you want to say to him or ask him?

> If I were to talk to Einstein, I would ask if all the things he did in his life were worth it. Of course Einstein made a giant leap for society, but would he rather live a more normal life instead of having to pay for his fame? Another question that I'd ask him is what he held in his life most dear to him. And if it was his wife, I'd ask if he would give up all of his theories just to have her back. I'd also ask him why his simplicity within his theories and nature was so important.

6. How did this reading selection change, add to, or reinforce your ideas about scientists in general, or about Albert Einstein specifically?

> I think that reading this selection greatly reinforced my ideas about Albert Einstein specifically. What I already knew about Einstein had already proved to be true in the story. However, I also learned how Einstein was able to become such a genius. It was mainly his beliefs about beauty and the world and how simplicity is the root to all complicated things. I never thought this to be true before the story, I had always believed that Einstein was incredible because he was of sheer brilliance and smarts.

High

Student A

7. This is your page to tell anything else you want about your understanding of this reading selection—what it means to you, what it reminds you of, how it relates to your own life, or whatever else you think is important about the reading selection.

After having read this selection, I think I've reinforced my views on life. I've realized that a person can be successful without having to give up your connection with the world. I learned about how Einstein was a finely tuned instrument that harmonized with the world to make beautiful music. Einstein has become a symbol of true dedication that has committed his whole life in the areas of science. As much as I wish I could be like Einstein, I also feel sympathy for him and the sadness that he felt when his ideas were abused. I have also found a new way of thinking and believing through reading this story. I've realized that a person has got to keep things simple and has got to work with the balance of time and of the universe, in order to accomplish things. But basically, I've learned that working within the essentials of life is the most important goal.

Commentary for High Exemplar

This reader demonstrates insight, discernment, and perception as she constructs meaning and reflects on the implications of Banesh Hoffmann's biographical sketch of his friend Albert Einstein. A careful analysis of her responses shows evidence of nearly all of the elements of a reading performance of the highest order: the reader is clearly intellectually engaged with the text as she speculates, explores divergent possibilities, and considers its complexities.

For this student, Einstein will never again be the same one-dimensional figure he was before she completed this assessment. In an impressive paper, this reader moves from a score of questions and comments written in the margins during her reading of the text to a sequence of insightful, discerning, and perceptive responses to the questions and activities that follow.

The marginal notations show her intellectual engagement with the text through challenging comments that raise questions, make judgments, ponder ambiguities, play with the language ("What's the difference between composing and creating?"), and speculate about Einstein's "scientifically religious" mind and character. She expresses appreciation for the explanation of surface tension: "I always wondered about the raindrops on a windowpane." She continually fills in gaps with plausible assumptions and an awareness of nuances.

Throughout the entire assessment, the reader lets us know that she has learned something. She begins her response to the first question with "Originally, I thought of Einstein as a prestigious and notable person that thought of basically impossible, but true, theories." "After having read this," she continues, "I discovered that Einstein was much more than a scientist and mathematician." She explores these ideas throughout the rest of the paper, responding to specific questions, but also continuing her own reflections about Einstein.

This reader extends her understanding of the text to make global connections based on her own understanding of today's culture. "To my generation, Einstein would never seem a simplistic man. . . ." Her final response is an exploration of both personal and universal implications of the text: "I learned . . . a new way of thinking and believing . . . that a person has got to keep things simple and has got to work with the balance of time and of the universe in order to accomplish things."

Sophisticated thinking strategies enable this student to make connections with ideas in the text and reflect on how they fit into her own understanding. She remains open to additional information as she reads, periodically articulating a newly developed level of understanding. Although many high papers will cluster their strengths in a few of the questions, this reader uses every opportunity to continue her reflective reading. As you look carefully at this paper, remember that you are reading the thoughts and ideas that an eighth-grade student was able to write down within the time constraints of one classroom period. It is an impressive performance.

Student B Middle

The responses of Student B were judged using the following rubric for middle readers. The score was based on the marginal notes that appear in the righthand column that runs alongside the story, as well as the responses to questions 1–7, which follow. A summary commentary appears at the end of Student B's responses.

R u b r i c   (Compare with High Rubric on page 32.)

Cognition: Readers in the middle range process print fluently. Middle readers, while confident, rarely take risks. They accept the text without exploring multiple possibilities of meaning. They tend to present their understanding of a text as fixed and rarely revise their interpretation as they reread and as additional information becomes available.

Rhetoric: Middle readers sometimes challenge or question the text. They may raise questions and may agree or disagree without explaining their reactions.

Linguistics/Conventions: Middle readers fill in some gaps in a text, making assumptions about unstated causes or motivations or drawing meaning from cues in the text. They usually differentiate between literal and figurative meanings. They may recognize real or seeming contradictions, but are sometimes distracted by these contradictions and by ambiguities. They demonstrate a thoughtful understanding of the whole work.

Themes/Ideas: Middle readers develop connections with and among texts. They usually connect their understanding of the text to their own experience and knowledge and sometimes to other texts. When directed, these readers may generate, validate, expand, and/or reflect on their ideas about the text, but with less depth. These readers tend to paraphrase or retell, often thoroughly and purposefully. They also see, however, a more general significance in or wider application of the literal facts of the text. They present a plausible and sometimes thoughtful interpretation..

---

1. **What are your thoughts and feelings about what you have read? Take a few minutes to write your ideas.**

My thoughts are that Einstein is a great man. His thinking ability is wonderful. I would have never thought about why your feet sink in the sand when it's dry and when wet it doesn't. As you see he had a logic explanation for his question. I feel if he had given up he would have been nothing but he kept trying so he was successful. People thought he was dumb but as he grew older he showed them that he could do anything he wanted and was accepted to Princeton.

2. Think about Einstein as a person and a scientist. In the split "profile" and below, use symbols, images, drawings, and/or words to give your ideas about Einstein the person and Einstein the scientist.

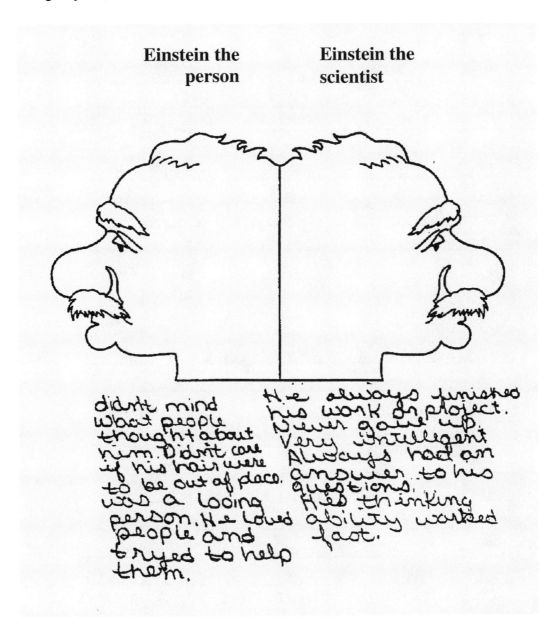

Einstein the person

Einstein the scientist

didn't mind what people thought about him. Didn't care if his hair were to be out of place. was a loving person. He loved people and tryed to help them.

He always finishes his work or project. Never gave up. Very intellegent. Always had an answer to his questions. His thinking ability worked fast.

3. Explain how the symbols, images, drawings, and/or words in your "profiles" represent your ideas about Einstein.

as a person:

He helped out the children on their carols to help buy Christmas presents. He wasn' a selfeconcious man he didn't care if he looked good but he felt good inside. He took good care of his belongings so they wouldn't get ruined.

as a scientist:

Einstein was a very hard worker, he always finished his projects and found a logic explanation for them all he was proved wrong he proved himselve right and never gave up If Einstein had a question he would answer it himselve. His abilities were fabulous considering him being a slow learner when being young

4. Think about Einstein the scientist and Einstein the person. Choose an example from the reading selection that shows how Einstein's personal characteristics affected him as a scientist.

> Einstein was a patient man and loved to work with people, to help them out. As you can see he had to of been patient because he had to let the ideas go to his head then think how to explain it. Well it was kind of like that when he helped the children with the caroling. Instead of giving them money he gave them something better, another helper. He was patient with them and played at their speed.

5. Based on your reading, if you were going to talk to Einstein, what would you want to say to him or ask him?

> I would want to thank him for giving us farmul we use in our Math and for giving us light. I would ask him how these ideas were thought of and how he did it.

43

Student B

6. How did this reading selection change, add to, or reinforce your ideas about scientists in general, or about Albert Einstein specifically?

> This changed my bad thought about scientist because they just don't invent things that kill other people but they make things that help us.

7. This is your page to tell anything else you want about your understanding of this reading selection—what it means to you, what it reminds you of, how it relates to your own life, or whatever else you think is important about the reading selection.

> This helped me realize that it doesn't necessarily mean that people at a young age aren't fast learners their going to be like that forever. Eventually they will start catch up and will pass everyone up. Also it's not right to laugh at people if they don't know how to read, instead help them. You never know they might become smarter than you and then see who will be laughing. So what I've learned is if a person isn't smart help them out don't put them aside!

Commentary for Middle Exemplar

This paper demonstrates a thoughtful, purposeful reading. The reader shows an understanding of the whole text and, even though she rarely takes risks, she stays focused on the task, each response expressing her understanding of what this text means and what it means in her life.

The reader draws some thoughtful connections in the margin notes. Even though these comments are primarily paraphrases or simple conclusions, she makes some observations that contribute to her later understanding, as in the comment "After his wifes death he was sad but didn't stop working he pushed hisselfe harder."

The conclusions this reader draws definitely go beyond literal responses. We can see how her first reading helped set her understanding when we look at a margin notation ("He worried about failing. But if it did he would try again.") and compare it to a later comment: "I feel if he had given up he would have been nothing but he kept trying so he was successful." Her initial margin note "He didn't care about what happened to his hair" is echoed in a later statement "He wasn't a self-concious man he didn't care if he looked good. . . ." These comments show that this reader established her understanding early in her reading and used the rest of the questions to reiterate these ideas.

As is typical in midrange responses, this reader shows that she sees wider applications of the literal facts of a text although she does so with less depth than in a high paper. This paper demonstrates glimpses of general significance in such comments as "This helped me realize that it doesn't necessarily mean that if people at a young age aren't fast learners their going to be like that forever."

While reading this paper, it is important to remember that we are reading first draft responses, enabling us to see the processes of understanding as they unfold. When we read these papers, we are not judging mastery of conventions. The responses in this performance match the middle-level description by being a combination of summary statements mixed with thoughtful conclusions.

Student C — Low

The responses of Student C were judged using the following rubric for low readers. The score was based on the student's responses to questions 1–7, which follow. You will notice that the student did not answer all of the questions. In addition, the student did not make marginal notes. A summary commentary appears at the end of the student's responses.

Rubric   (Compare with High Rubric on page 32 and Middle Rubric on page 40.)

Cognition: Low-range readers tend to have some problems processing print. They devote so much attention to turning the code into meaning that they have little time left for interpretations, asking questions, and so forth.

Rhetoric: Low readers seldom ask questions of a text or offer meaningful evaluations of what they read. They tend to abandon sections of text or become entangled in difficult sections of a text.

Linguistics/Conventions: Low readers have some basic sense of sentence structure and conventions, but tend to be vague about parts of overall text structure.

Themes/Ideas: A limited reading performance indicates that readers construct partial and/or reductive meanings for a text. They may demonstrate a superficial understanding of parts of the text. They demonstrate a reductive meaning for the text by overgeneralizing or oversimplifying but seem unable to grasp the whole. Low readers develop few or no connections with texts. They may, as they recognize some idea, continue to write or draw, but their responses will appear to have only a tangential relevance to the text.

Student C

1. What are your thoughts and feelings about what you have read? Take a few minutes to write your ideas.

> I Feel that aBrlt estine was
> took the ~~sc~~ wroers way Be
> cause He Did not want to Hurt any
> ~~~~ iBoDv at all

2. Think about Einstein as a person and a scientist. In the split "profile" and below, use symbols, images, drawings, and/or words to give your ideas about Einstein the person and Einstein the scientist.

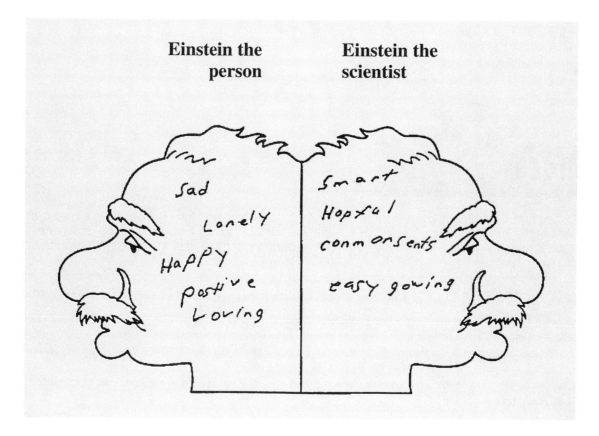

Einstein the person

Sad
Lonely
HaPPY
postive
Loving

Einstein the scientist

Smart
Hopful
conm onsents
easy gowing

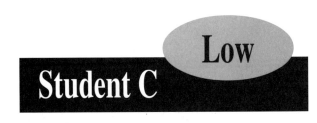

3. Explain how the symbols, images, drawings, and/or words in your "profiles" represent your ideas about Einstein.

as a person:

He cared uBout people aloct and
didn't realy want to Hurt anyBoDy

as a scientist:

4. Think about Einstein the scientist and Einstein the person. Choose an example from the reading selection that shows how Einstein's personal characteristics affected him as a scientist.

He cared aBout peope So HetLelpeb
people wIth His costriBorts toSciencs
But was taken wroungly made the Amtomic
BomB By axcedent

5. Based on your reading, if you were going to talk to Einstein, what would you want to say to him or ask him?

what Do you think ofSisty now
and what would you do to Helpit

Commentary for Low Exemplar

In this low performance, the reader presents a limited awareness of the meaning of the text. He does show evidence of reading, but he expresses his understanding in broad, sweeping, reductive statements. The reader focuses on the fact that ". . . he did not want to hurt any body at all." He repeats this observation, along with other statements echoing the same conclusions about Einstein. He makes no connections to the text either from his own experiences or from previous knowledge.

This reader would benefit from extended conversations about the texts that he reads, both with his peers and with a teacher who could probe for greater depth of understanding. At this time, however, the reader demonstrates only a partial, limited understanding of the Einstein sketch.

NOTE: The third student did not respond to questions 6 and 7.

Connections to Standards

	STANDARDS											
On-Demand	1	2	3	4	5	6	7	8	9	10	11	12
Embedded	1	2	3	4	5	6	7	8	9	10	11	12

In an on-demand situation, responses to literary texts require students to apply a range of strategies to comprehend, interpret, evaluate, and critique texts (1, 2, 3, 6). When embedded in classroom instruction, responses might also include visual representations (4) and texts might include such nonprint sources as films and television and radio broadcasts (1). Depending on the texts being read or viewed and the responses being elicited or offered, reponding to literary texts can help students develop an understanding of and respect for diversity (9). Students whose first language is not English can use their first language to develop understanding of texts (10). Students can use responses to literary texts to accomplish their own purposes, such as developing and exploring an interpretation of a self-selected novel (12).

Task

In reading records, students were asked to provide evidence that they had read:

- at least twenty-five books (or their equivalent in articles, newspapers, or textbooks) in the course of a year (knowing about);
- materials that are age-appropriate and high-quality, e.g., chosen from recognized reading lists (knowing about);
- a well-balanced selection of materials from classic and contemporary literature and from public discourse (documentary essays, news analyses, editorials) (knowing about);
- at least three different kinds (genres) of printed materials (for example, novels, biographies, magazine articles) (knowing that);
- works of at least five different authors (knowing about);
- at least four books (or book equivalents) about one issue, or in one genre, or by a single author (or a combination of all of these) (knowing that).

Exemplar High

Rubric

The reader meets all of the necessary requirements listed in the task (see above).

Commentary

This eighth grader has documented a prodigious amount of reading, meeting the requirement of twenty-five books or book equivalents by totaling over 9,410 pages read. The works listed are both high-quality and challenging, including works of popular adult fiction (e.g., *Patriot Games, Roots*). While the student has read extensively in fantasy and contemporary fiction, few works of classic literature are represented here. No reading in public discourse is documented. The student has read at

---

Book Log for
As of May 1, 1995
Covering my Eighth-Grade Year

<u>David Brin</u>
Earth - Spectacular and facinating book. Character development excellent, story excellent!!   700–800 pgs
The Postman - carries a great message and reads very quickly   400–500 pgs
Sundiver - Great adventure and science fiction mix first in trilogy   350 pgs
Startide Rising - suspenseful, fantasy-like thriller! (second in trilogy)   640 pgs
The Uplift War - Same excellent thought, writing, character development as all others. David Brin is fantastic!! (third in trilogy)   640 pgs

<u>Anne McCaffrey</u>
All the Weyrs of Pern - Fantastic book that continues the epic story of Pern, one of my favorites!   approx. 700 pgs
The Renegades of Pern - Great quality and character development, shows you a totally different side of the other Pern tales.   approx. 700 pgs
Dinosaur Planet - I love this story, it has the technical and exciting parts to make a great story.   300–400 pgs
Get Off the Unicorn - A book with many short stories and works of writing that Anne herself has put together. She also includes many stories about her past experiences and feelings.   600 pgs

Paper continued on page 50

least three different kinds of printed materials, including fantasy, historical fiction, and short story. The student has read the works of more than five different writers and has read in depth in the area of fantasy, concentrating on the authors David Brin and Anne McCaffrey. Brief comments about each work listed show that the student has engaged with the texts read. For example, the student's comment on *The Dolphins of Pern* shows that he is considering issues of authors' craft. The comment accompanying Edgar Allan Poe's "The Pit and the Pendulum" suggests that this student is aware of and monitoring his reading processes. This reading record is commendable for quantity and depth, but this student could benefit from broadening his reading to include some public discourse (commentaries on issues, issue books).

Ship Who Searched - Just finished reading it! Also by Mercedes Lackey; a joint production between the two authors. I loved it! You can tell it has some other feeling besides Anne McCaffrey and I'm not sure if I like the feeling. But, still an awesome book.   300 pgs

The Dolphins of Pern - Great book!! It think it will not be the end of the story of Pern. It seems that every time Anne decides to end the amazing series, another book appears. Comparing her style of writing about dolphins and David Brin's, I find that both show the intelligence of the mammals but David seems to go in-depth a little more in their habits and nuances, but I could tell you the different characteristics and feelings Anne's have so I don't know what to say!

Alex Haley
Roots - Amazing tale!! I relished in the beauty of knowledge and writing. 800 pgs

Andre Norton
The Mark Of The Cat - I love her writing!! This tale is so increasingly wonderful that I have read it three times this year!   400 pgs

Tom Clancy
Patriot Games - An obvious win! I loved it and couldn't put it down until it was over! Reads very fast!   400 pgs

Brian Jaques
Redwall - A tale almost like the Rats of Nymn. The character development was so fun! I loved the great things these animals could think of and do. 300 pgs

Patrice Kindl
Owl in Love - A great story that is very easy to read. I love the events that take place and the ending is so filling.   250 pgs

Mary Zamberno
Journeyman Wizard - Fun and exciting book to read. I started with the manuscript, fixed-spelling, written-in-words version and moved to the finished hardbound version. Both were a joy to read.   200 pgs

Gary Paulsen
The River - I had heard how wonderful it was and that I should read it (when it first came out a few years ago) so I finally got around to it. Wow! Does Brian ever give up?   200–300 pgs

Edgar Allen Poe
The Pit and the Pendulum - I first became interested in Poe, when we read one of his stories in our Language Arts Book. This came with a tape. I found that reading it before listening to the tape is the best. I also learned that I do not retain at least most of the story if I read and listen at the same time. That is not totally true it's just that I become either involved in one part or the other and lose my place in the book, or block out something important on the tape.   little over 50 pgs

Mark Twain
The Aventures of Tom Sawyer - Fun and exciting book to read. Reminds me of all the normal, troublesome kids you see on television and wish you could have had as friends for only a while.   140 pgs

Total of 20 Books read
With over 9410 pages

7th Grade Reading Journal

	DATE	TITLE	AUTHOR	GENRE	RATING 5=excellent 4=good 3=satisfactory 2=limited 1=poor
1	10-4-94	Number the Stars		Historical fic.	5
2	10-14-94	Journey to America	Sonia Levitin	Historical fic	3
3	11-4-94	Mama Lets Dance	Patricia Hermes	Fiction	4
4	12-7-94	~~~~	~~~~	~~~~	~~~~
4	12-7-94	Tiger Eyes	Judy Blume	Fiction	4
5	1-3-95	There's a girl in my hammerlock		Fiction	4
6	1-17-95	Ms. Quarterback	Francis Pascels	Fiction	5
7	2-28-95	Black Beauty	Anna Sewell	Fiction	4
8	3-1-95	Greg Louganis	People Magazine	Magazine Artical	5
9	3-1-95	Nicole Bobek	People Magazine	Magazine Artical	4
10	3-2-95	"I almost starved myself to death"	People	Magazine Artical	5
11	3-24-95	The year of the Panda		Fiction	4
12	4-25-95	Help Me		Non Fiction	4
13	5-9-95	Jacob's Rescue	Malka Drucker	Non Fiction	4
		The Outsiders	C Hinton		5

R u b r i c

The reader falls below the requirements for high achievement, listed in the task requirements. Middle readers tend to read ten to fifteen books and to limit the range (genre, literary and nonliterary).

C o m m e n t a r y

This seventh-grade student has documented a moderate amount of reading, including about ten complete books. Several entries on the reading list consist of short articles from People magazine. The majority of works listed are of adequate quality and age-appropriate. The works listed represent a fairly limited range of classic and contemporary literature, e.g., *Number the Stars* and *Black Beauty*. The range of nonfiction reading is also limited. No reading of public discourse is documented here. The student *has* read in at least three different genres, e.g., historical fiction, magazine articles, and young adult fiction, but the overall quality of the reading is both adequate and unremarkable. The student has read at least five different authors, but does not provide evidence of having read in depth in any of the areas suggested in the task.

Exemplar — Low

Rubric

The low reader either reads very little, zero to ten books, or else reads ten to twenty pieces which are of uncertain quality and uncertain form (article or book? joke book or short story?). The low reader may not be a fluent reader.

1. Canyons – A story of two boys in diff+t canyons.
2. Sancho – The story of a cattle drive.
3. Christmas day in the morning – A story of memorys.
4. The trouble with television – A story of the cons of tv.
5. When I heard the song bird sing – A story of caring.
6. Mushrooms – A poem of how mushrooms are.
7. Harriet Tubman: Guide to freedom – A story of Harriet Tubman.
8. Crime on mars – A story of a crime on mars.
9. The Pearl – A story of a hidden pearl and the fight to find it.
10. Paul Reveres ride – The story of Paul Revere.
11. HBO Schedule of Feb. 18 – Reading what was coming on TV.
12. Gettysburg Address – Lincoln's most famous speech.
13. O captain my captain – A story of after Lincoln's death.

Commentary

This eighth-grade student has documented reading thirteen texts, including several poems, a television schedule, and the text of a speech. Since the student has referred to almost every entry as a "story," it is difficult to determine which entries really are "stories" and which are not. Some good-quality works are listed here, but this reading record falls far short of the task's requirements in quantity, breadth, and depth. The works of five different authors are represented on this list, but there is no evidence that the student has read in depth in any of the dimensions described in the task.

Connections to Standards

	STANDARDS											
On-Demand	1	2	3	4	5	6	7	8	9	10	11	12
Embedded	1	2	3	4	5	6	7	8	9	10	11	12

The breadth of reading requirement challenges the student to apply a range of reading strategies for comprehending, interpreting, evaluating, and critiquing texts (1, 2, 3, 6).

T a s k

This section is designed to show teachers some useful ways of using visual representation in the classroom. Teachers asked students to use graphics to summarize information. Not all of the exemplars on pages 53 - 61 were scored. We encourage teachers, students, and parents to discuss the samples and to determine which ranking might be appropriate.

TOPIC 1: Carmen's and Matt's graphic organizers show how visual representation can be used to express prior knowledge.

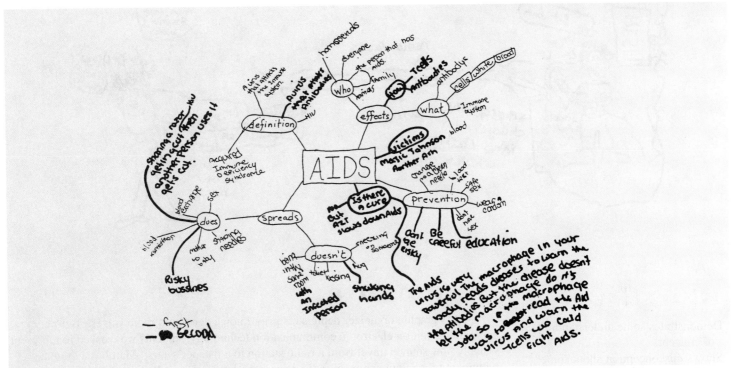

Graphic organizers on pages 53 through 56 from Irwin-Devitis, L., and Pease, D. (1995). Using graphic organizers for learning and assessment in middle level classrooms. *Middle School Journal 26*(5), 57–64.

Commentary

Carmen's graphic organizer depicts her prior knowledge about AIDS (thin lines) and what she learned from a unit of classroom instruction on AIDS (thick lines). The teacher provided the basic organizers of the definition of AIDS, its effects, its prevention, and its spread.

R u b r i c

Demonstrates a high level of prior knowledge about subject.

Uses accurate terms in notations.

Uses size of circle and point to distinguish between major concepts and secondary concepts.

Combines timeline and concept map.

Uses writing to summarize understanding of solution and uses visual map to represent relationships.

Exemplar

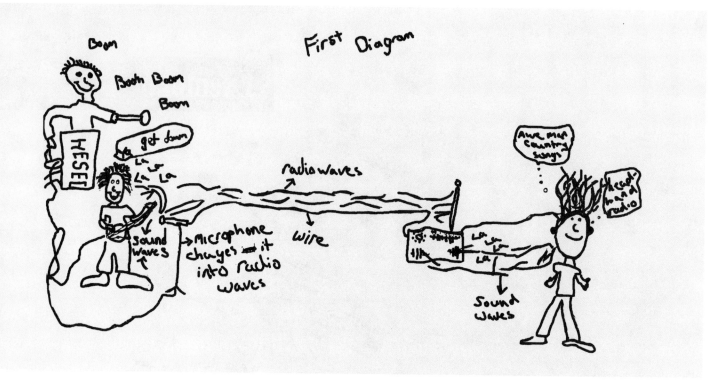

Rubric

Demonstrates some understanding of concept.

Shows misconception about some components of subject.

Pictures do not represent concepts.

Mixes up two functions of graphics—the drawing of a picture to tell a story and the map or matrix to show relationships.

Commentary

Matt's graphic organizer depicts his prior knowledge about radio waves. Before beginning a unit on electronic communication technology, students were asked to represent visually how sounds travel from a radio station to a listener's ears. Matt has a dramatic picture, but the relationships of radio waves and music or sound are unclear. One reason for the confusion is the absence of a standard graphic to stand for radio waves. Matt has presented a drawing of an event, but he has not presented a visual representation of relationships.

TOPIC 2: Matt's and Erica's graphic organizers show how visual representation can be used to make both personal and inter-disciplinary connections.

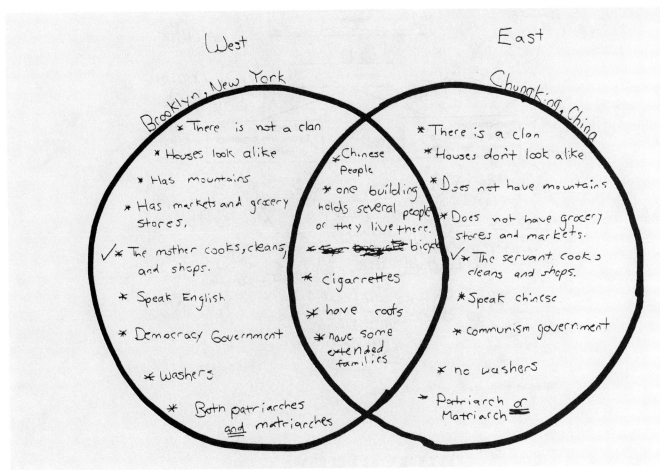

West

Brooklyn, New York

* There is not a clan
* Houses look alike
* Has mountains
* Has markets and grocery stores.
✓* The mother cooks, cleans, and shops.
* Speak English.
* Democracy Government
* Washers
* Both patriarches and matriarches

*Chinese People
* one building holds several people or they live there.
~~* For bicycle~~ bicycle
* cigarettes
* have roots
* have some extended families

East

Chunaking, China

* There is a clan
* Houses don't look alike
* Does not have mountains
* Does not have grocery stores and markets.
✓* The servant cooks cleans and shops.
* Speak chinese
* communism government
* no washers
* Patriarch or Matriarch

Commentary

Matt's graphic organizer shows interdisciplinary connections. After reading *In the Year of the Boar and Jackie Robinson,* by Bette Bao Lord, Matt uses a Venn diagram to compare the two main settings in the novel.

55

Exemplar

Erica

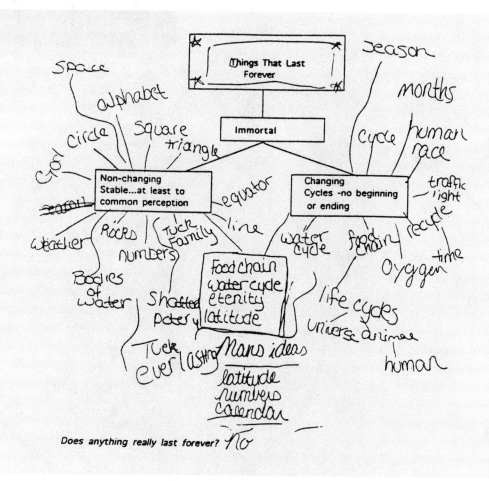

Things That Last Forever

Immortal

Non-changing
Stable...at least to
common perception

Changing
Cycles -no beginning
or ending

space
alphabet
God circle
square
triangle
seasons
weather
Rocks
numbers
Tuck
Family
equator
line
water cycle
food chain
recycle
Oxygen
time
Bodies of water
Shattered
Pottery
Food chain
water cycle
etenity
latitude
life cycles
universe
animal
human
Tuck everlasting
Mans ideas
latitude
numbers
calendar

season
months
cycle
human race
traffic light

Does anything really last forever? No

Rubric

Uses knowledge from several
  disciplines.
Demonstrates an understanding of
  the major concepts.
Differentiates between natural
  occurrences and human inventions.
Shows relationships clearly.
Seems to makes personal connections to major concepts.

Commentary

Erica's graphic organizer shows an understanding of relationships. Students read *Tuck Everlasting*, by Natalie Babbit, and used mapping to represent theme and symbolism. The teacher provided the structure (typed blocks).

TOPIC 3: Chris's and Sara's graphs of "significant positives and negatives" show how visual representation can be used to represent experience.

Exemplar

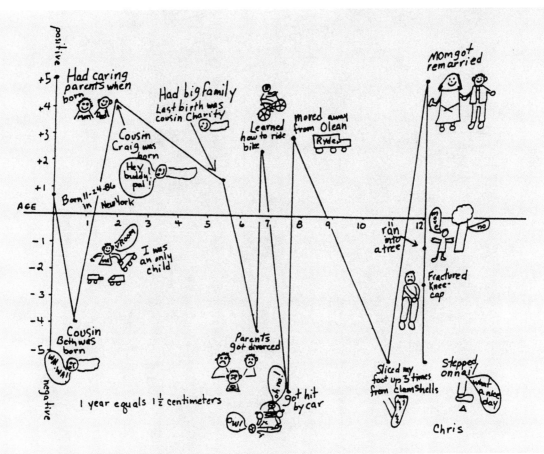

Graphic organizers on pages 57 and 58 from Linda Rief, *Seeking Diversity: Language Arts with Adolescents*. (Portsmouth, N.H.: Heinemann, 1992).

Commentary

Students brainstormed the best and worst things that had ever happened to them and then represented them on a graph. Chris's timeline is organized by age in years. The positives and negatives are organized around the up-down scale on the left, and the time scale is organized around ages marked on the line across the middle. Chris gives a scale at the bottom of the graph: "1 year equals 1´ centimeters."

Rubric

The graph uses two principles—left to right representing time and above or below representing positive or negative experiences. (See notations on the right and on the line.) Distance above and below the line is also used as a notation of degrees of positive or negative. The pictures add helpful icons to the representation.

Exemplar

Sara

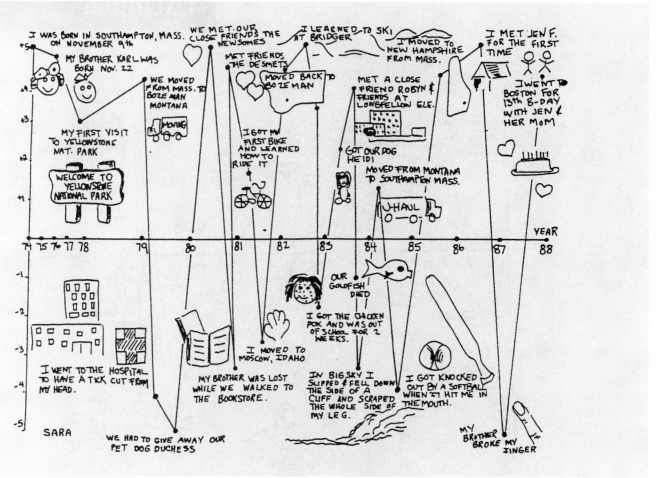

I WAS BORN IN SOUTHAMPTON, MASS. ON NOVEMBER 9th

MY BROTHER KARL WAS BORN NOV. 22

WE MET OUR CLOSE FRIENDS THE NEWSOMES

I LEARNED TO SKI AT BRIDGER

I MOVED TO NEW HAMPSHIRE FROM MASS.

I MET JEN F. FOR THE FIRST TIME

WE MOVED FROM MASS. TO BOZEMAN MONTANA

MET FRIENDS THE DESMETS

MOVED BACK TO BOZEMAN

MET A CLOSE FRIEND ROBYN & FRIENDS AT LONGFELLOW ELE.

I WENT TO BOSTON FOR 13th B-DAY WITH JEN & HER MOM

MY FIRST VISIT TO YELLOWSTONE NAT. PARK

I GOT MY FIRST BIKE AND LEARNED HOW TO RIDE IT

GOT OUR DOG HEIDI

MOVED FROM MONTANA TO SOUTHAMPTON MASS.

WELCOME TO YELLOWSTONE NATIONAL PARK

UHAUL

YEAR

74 75 76 77 78   79   80   81   82   83   84   85   86   87   88

OUR GOLDFISH DIED

I WENT TO THE HOSPITAL TO HAVE A TICK CUT FROM MY HEAD.

I GOT THE CHICKEN POX AND WAS OUT OF SCHOOL FOR 2 WEEKS.

I MOVED TO MOSCOW, IDAHO

MY BROTHER WAS LOST WHILE WE WALKED TO THE BOOKSTORE.

IN BIG SKY I SLIPPED & FELL DOWN THE SIDE OF A CLIFF AND SCRAPED THE WHOLE SIDE OF MY LEG.

I GOT KNOCKED OUT BY A SOFTBALL WHEN IT HIT ME IN THE MOUTH.

SARA

WE HAD TO GIVE AWAY OUR PET DOG DUCHESS

MY BROTHER BROKE MY FINGER

Rubric

The graph uses two principles—left to right representing time (calendar years) and above or below the line representing positive or negative.

Notations are also used to express degrees of distance above (positive) or below (negative).

The pictures are helpful icons, adding smiles and frowns to the representation.

Commentary

Sara's timeline is organized by calendar years and by degrees above and below. Her story appears never to have had level periods. The graphic is organized around the positive-negative on the left and the year scale across the middle of the graphic.

TOPIC 4: The students were asked to show how visual representation can be integrated with text in the presentation of directions. Students were asked to give directions from their school to their homes by mapping and writing directions. Because all students were familiar with the neighborhood and because home addresses would have made the problem too easy, students were asked not to use their home addresses as a point of reference. During the drafting stage, students exchanged maps for editing.

Exemplar **High**

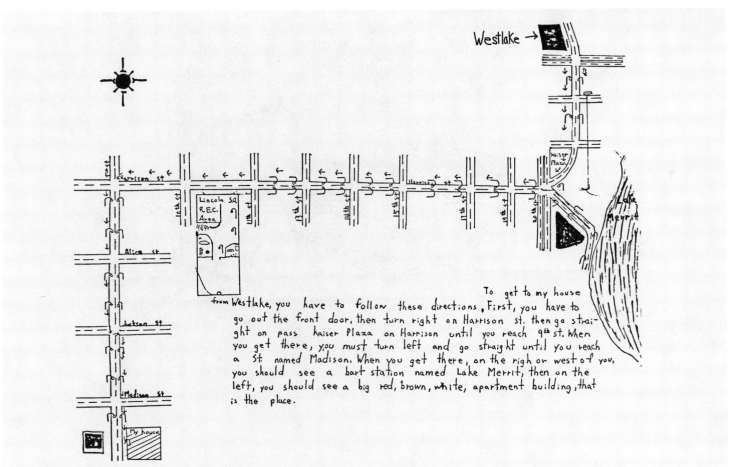

To get to my house from Westlake, you have to follow these directions. First, you have to go out the front door, then turn right on Harrison st. then go straight on pass kaiser Plaza on Harrison until you reach 9th st. When you get there, you must turn left and go straight until you reach a st. named Madison. When you get there, on the righ or west of you, you should see a bart station named Lake Merrit, then on the left, you should see a big red, brown, white, apartment building, that is the place.

R u b r i c

The notations for the streets are clear and complete. All details are provided.

The text is clear and complete. Each street is shown.

Notational compass in upper left provides direction and arrows indicate direction of movement.

Exemplar

Middle

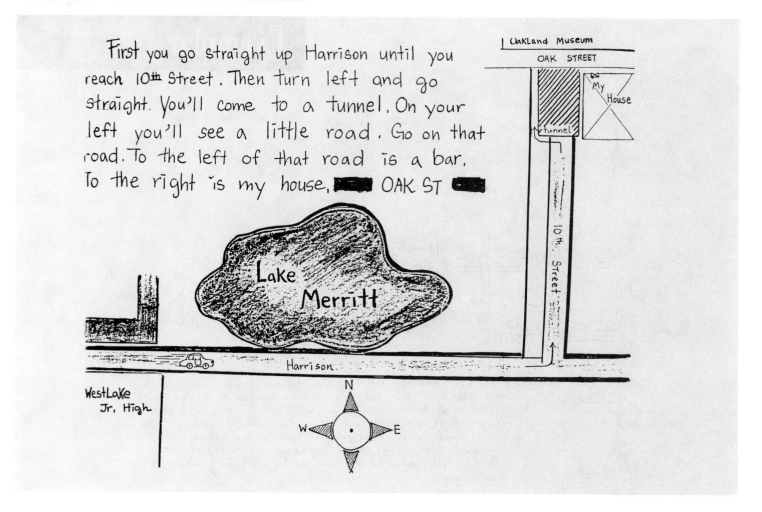

First you go straight up Harrison until you reach 10ᵗʰ Street. Then turn left and go straight. You'll come to a tunnel. On your left you'll see a little road. Go on that road. To the left of that road is a bar. To the right is my house. ▬ OAK ST ▬

Lake Merritt

Oakland Museum
OAK STREET

My House

tunnel

10ᵗʰ Street

Harrison

WestLake Jr. High

N
W • E
S

R u b r i c

Orients reader with compass symbol at bottom.

Provides only key landmarks on map. Many details are missing.

Provides only key decision points in written directions. Does not show all key points in written directions on map and does not provide an idea of distance to be traveled.

Map accurately represents written instructions.

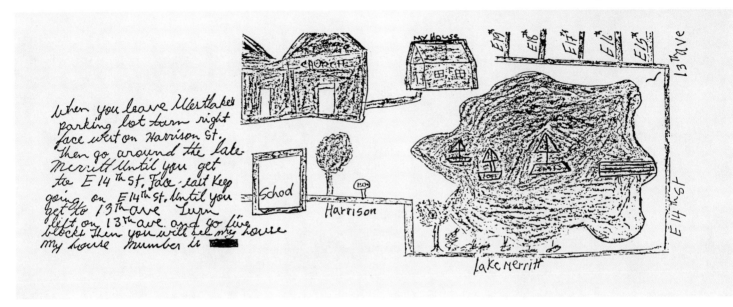

When you leave Westlake's parking lot turn right face west on Harrison St. Then go around the lake Merritt Until you get to E 14th st. Face east Keep going on E 14th St. Until you get to 13th ave Turn left on 13th ave. and go five blocks. Then you will see my house my house number is ▮▮▮

Rubric

Uses written directional cues (E = East?) but provides no directional symbols on map.

Illustrations and distances on map are out of scale.

School seems to sit in the middle of Harrison or Harrison passes under it.

Written text has a few errors (spelling) and is sometimes too general.

Writing leaves out essential details.

Connections to Standards

	STANDARDS											
On-Demand	1	2	3	4	5	6	7	8	9	10	11	12
Embedded	1	2	3	4	5	6	7	8	9	10	11	12

When embedded in classroom instruction, visual representations offer students a variety of possibilities for responding to literary and non-literary, print and nonprint texts (1, 2). Visual representation can become a strategy for comprehending, interpreting, evaluating, and appreciating texts (3). In addition, visual representations, such as concepts maps, Venn diagrams, and illustrations can play an important role in the development of a piece of writing (4, 5, 6). Visual representation, such as charts, graphs, and multimedia presentations, can also serve as a vehicle for creating and communicating knowledge (7, 8). Students can use visual representation to accomplish their own purposes (12), such as designing brochures and enhancing oral presentations.

Portfolios

The section that follows contains excerpts from the portfolios of three middle school students—Mimi, Reggie, and Greg. From each portfolio we have selected only a few pieces for inclusion here. In some cases, we show only excerpts of pieces, but enough to give you a general idea of the quality of the whole piece. The purpose of this section is to give you an idea of what a collection of a student's work—as opposed to a single sample— may reveal about that student's learning and accomplishments in English language arts.

The selections from Mimi's, Reggie's, and Greg's portfolios represent a range of levels of performance—high (Mimi), middle (Reggie), and low (Greg). We are not suggesting that Mimi's work represents the very best that has been or could ever be done. Likewise, we are not suggesting that Greg's work represents some absolute minimum level. Our intent is to represent some of the range of performances which English teachers encounter in today's heterogeneously grouped classes and to represent the judgments which teachers make about the levels of achievement in those performances.

Mimi, Reggie, and Greg are students in different classrooms from different parts of the country. When they assembled their portfolios, they were participating in the second year of the field trial of the New Standards English language arts portfolio system,[1] which was at that time managed by the Literacy Unit at NCTE. This system requires students to show examples of their best work and to follow a common "menu" in putting together their portfolios. This menu was based on the NCTE/IRA standards. Among the required items were:

- evidence of reading accomplishment in literature, informational materials, and public discourse;
- evidence of quantity, range, and depth in reading;
- evidence of writing in a variety of genres or modes (e.g., argument or persuasion, narration, report of information);
- evidence of speaking, listening, and viewing;
- an introductory reflective essay describing what the contents of the portfolio suggest about growth in English language arts;
- a table of contents.

Mimi's, Reggie's, and Greg's portfolios were scored by teachers in their local states and districts, and then sent to a national meeting, where they were scored by teachers from across the country. Many of these portfolios were scored again by NCTE teachers in NCTE's national meetings. Some of these teachers' judgments and comments appear in the rubric-based marginal comments and the summary commentaries at the end of each portfolio. The summaries discuss the degree to which the portfolio as a whole represents achievement in the three ways of knowing (i.e., knowing that, knowing how, knowing about) and the four domains of English language arts described in the introduction to this book (i.e., cognition, rhetoric, linguistics/conventions, and cultural themes and ideas).

Throughout this section, "Connections to Standards" appear in the margins. Connections between relevant portions of the NCTE/IRA standards and individual entries are shown here. These are not the *only* possible connections that could be made between the standards and the portfolio entries; they are, however, particularly salient connections.

The work that you see here will undoubtedly prompt you to ask many questions about the work itself and about the circumstances leading to and surrounding the production of the final portfolio. We hope that you will pursue these questions with your colleagues and that you will understand that we cannot address here all the provocative issues raised when we study, interpret, and evaluate student work.

---

[1] New Standards is a partnership of approximately twenty states and urban districts working to build an assessment system that measures students' progress toward achieving a set of standards (also being developed by New Standards).

Portfolios

Mimi

Reggie

Greg

Mimi compiled her portfolio at the end of her seventh-grade year. Her portfolio represents a selection of the work she completed over the course of the school year. We have selected only a few pieces to show you here. Some of the pieces are excerpts only. Note: The letters in the rubrics/commentaries should be matched with the letters in the margins of the student work, thereby showing the location of the features cited.

High

Reflective Essay

Task

Mimi was asked to include an introductory reflective essay on the contents of the portfolio (growth, goals).

Reading & Writing Self-Profile

A.

Throughout this 7th grade school year, I have improved in many ways and become more independent. This year has been like an awakening for me, and I've experienced so many things that I never even thought about when I was in elementary school. I've met new and different people, experienced major fear, depression, and akwardness, learned to switch classes, and signed up for new

B.

arts classes. All these events have enriched me as a person, and therefore as a writer. I've also desired to read books with more depth. 7th grade has changed me remarkably.

My English teacher,   taught my class how to compose high-quality papers. I've learned how to write process

C.

papers, areobic writing, journal entries, and book reports. From composing in these styles, I can now write superb introductions, body paragraphs, and conclusions.   gave us lessons on writing topic sentences, or those that introduce the subject to

D.

the beginning of a paragraph; and clinchers, a sentence that ends a paragraph. Now I'm more experienced with both. My spelling, punctuation, and grammer have always been excellent. I try to explain stories so the reader isn't confused. When writing book reports, I explain the plot, characters, and my feelings on the

E.

story. Before, I had to use sheets that told what questions to answer about the book, but now I can simply type on my computer

F.

my feelings and relating experiences for a book report. For

process papers, I follow the Peer Helps and sentence structure sheets fully to improve my paper. The result is more interesting, clear sentences. I'm excellent at expository writing.

Rubric / Commentary

A. In the opening paragraph, the student establishes theme of change and growth.
B. Makes connection between personal growth and growth in writing.
C. States specific characteristics of "high quality papers."
D. Understands reading/writing connection.
E. Gives specific examples of progress in writing.
F. States strengths succinctly and uses correct terminology of the discipline (e.g., "expository writing").

Paper continued on page 66

G. States specific weaknesses.
H. Shows awareness of author's craft ("choppy" vs. "smooth and poetic").
I. Understands role of facts in fiction and the importance of knowing about a subject when writing about it.
J. States concrete goal for writing and specific strategies for achieving goal.
K. States specific example of growth in reading.
L. Understands importance of reading challenging works in a variety of genres.

Connections to Standards

Mimi demonstrates substantial achievement in:

• participating as a knowledgeable, reflective, creative, and critical member of a literacy community (11).

G.
H.
I.

A weakness I have is writing my own stories. I do very well in English, but by myself I want to write fictional stories, and it's harder for me. I try to have good description, but sometimes it turns out choppy, and not smooth and poetic like I want. I also need to learn more. When I'm writing a story and there's a part that is supposed to be fact, I don't know enough to be able to write about it. For example, if I want to make up a story about made-up creatures that live in the sea, I have to know at least a little about the real creatures that live in the sea. I would have to research to find out about various fish, their habitats, and how they would affect the made up characters in the story. I must know more about the world to write about it.

J.

My goal is to keep a journal and to write a short novel. During the summer or in 8th grade, I plan to write entries in a notebook. I'll write about situations that happen to me, my thoughts, and stories. From those journal ideas or others, I will write a fictional story. Keeping a journal can let me look back at what I've done and I'll be able to remember all my feelings and hopes. If I write a short story or novel, I will show it to my friends and   , my creative writing teacher from the first half of the school year. Twice, my work has been published in the   Journal, and I can enter in a short story so I will be able to get a copy of the journal.

K.

This year I've started to read a wider variety of books that have more depth to them. Book reports for English and my own aspiration prompt me to read more. The school library and my friends' recommendations have helped me to find some great fiction. At home, I have cleared my bookshelves of babyish books, and am starting to collect novels that appeal to my changing tastes. Right now I have fantasy, mystery, and romance books. The book reports   taught my class to do helped me evaluate and probe stories. We were given sheets with questions to ask ourselves to help us relate to the books we read. With more complex reading, I'll be able to think in a new way.

L.

M. Because I'm starting to read advanced novels, I can't understand many words. But I keep a small dictionary by my bed, so when I read at night, I can use it for reference. I've learned new words, and I hope to use them in my writing. Once I've mastered a large vocabulary, I will also be able to concentrate on the plot and motivations of characters in books I read. I sometimes get lost in elaborate paragraphs. For some of the passages, I wonder if I'm interpreting the plot correctly. Hopefully, by the next school year I will be able to expand my vocabulary and understand tangled context.

N. Reading and writing are connected, and I must improve both. By reading advanced novels, I will improve my vocabulary and will recognize different styles of writing. I can use interesting ideas and a strong vocabulary for my own writing. If I achieve my goals, I will be able to compose a novel by the end of the next school year. I learned how to write very successfully this year,

O. and I will carry that talent for my whole life.

> **M.** Discusses reading strategies and shows awareness of text structures.
> **N.** Closes effectively by connecting reading and writing, accomplishments and goals.
> **O.** Throughout paper, student shows excellent grasp of sentence structure, punctuation, capitalization, spelling, and various other conventions.

Task

Mimi was asked to show her accomplishments in reading literature.

Response to Literature

High

The Door in the Air and Other Stories

A. When my mom brought home a book she had gotten from the library for me, I thought it was a babyish children's book since it was short. The book, called The Door in the Air, by Margaret Mahy, was actually very wonderful, and I'm glad I read it. The stories were so true and beautiful, that the book was like a treasure.

B. The Door in the Air was a book composed of nine different tales of fantasy about wizards, castles, bridges, changes, and life. The way they were written gave each story an aura of truth. Each story told a meaning of life. One tale, The Two Sisters, told how two twin daughters were exact opposites. One was of light, the other darkness. But by the end, each daughter gave their ill mother an important gift. Another story was about two people who finally let themselves go to the wind. The Door in the Air taught about art, unexpectedness, and changes of the world.

C. One of the best stories in the book was called The Bridge Builder. It was about this traveler named Merlin who had a father who worked as a bridge builder. At first, to buy his children's christmas presents, he built practical bridges where people told him to build them. But after his children grew up, he built the bridges of his dreams, that were artistic masterpieces. The

Rubric/Commentary

A. In the introduction, the student gives insight into strategies for selecting books and summarizes personal response to text read.
B. Gives succinct summary of whole book.
C. Explores in depth one story, "The Bridge Builder."

Paper continued on page 68

D. Gives gist of plot, then explores symbolism of bridges and personal response to theme.

E. Analyzes, interprets, and evaluates literary texts.

F. Uses anecdote to explain connection between literacy in and out of school.

G. Vivid details and personal reflection upon significance of incident enhance effectiveness of anecdote.

H. Effectively summarizes theme in final sentence.

Connections to Standards

Mimi demonstrates substantial achievement in:

• reading literature to build an understanding of the many dimensions of human experience (2);

• applying a wide range of strategies to comprehend, interpret, evaluate, and appreciate texts (3).

D. bridges were in unusual places, one was over a volcano with harps as handrails, some were in forests over rivers, some contained beautiful caged birds and fish. There were hanging garden bridges and bridges built on the city on top of skyscrapers. But since people could not cross all the bridges or even cross them in the same way, the government was angry and soldiers were sent out to get Merlin's father. When they came to a forest, Merlin said a magic word, half made up, and his father turned into a bridge that helped the soldiers who were falling in the river. I thought that story was so beautiful. I believe in the principles of Merlin's father. Bridges are needed in unexpected places just for the reason that they're there. You can know a bridge is out there somewhere in the world and never find it. Or maybe it will just crumble. But it was there. The world is full of wonder, and

E. Merlin's father made odd bridges that suspended over rivers and add surprise to life. Merlin's father questioned if a man would be the same man he was before he crossed a bridge. Are we all the same people as we walk through time?, is what I ask. I also loved the idea of a bridge Merlin's father made. It was made of silver thread and mother of pearl and was to be crossed at midnight. When you crossed, you would walk into the next day. That idea is very appealing to me. Just by stepping across an overpass, you would walk onto the other side into a new day. This story told that by strolling across the bridges of the world, you would change somehow. The tale is about life - seasons, seconds; passing and changing.

F. I liked the story so much that I decided to tell it to my dad. It was a hot afternoon and I brought the straw mat out to sit on, and two books: The Door in the Air and another one called California Blue. My dad was outside, too, cleaning something. I decided to read my favorite tale, The Bridge Builder, for him. As he cleaned, I read, with much feeling as I really loved the story. I paused every few minutes to ask if he was listening, and repeated a few parts as necessary. Twice, my dad went inside the house to get some things. On the later trip, he brought back slices of watermelon. Then, my cat Silver jumped over the fence and rested himself in front of us. He looked so funny because he was laying on his stomach with his legs stretched out in back of him, and his eyes were mischievous as they always get when he goes outside. My dad spit watermelon seeds on Silver to annoy him, and Silver just lay there, contented, with dark brown seeds on his back. We were interupted four times when an employee of my mom's came in and when a guy opened the fence to ask if we wanted our lawn mowed (we didn't). Then my mom asked me if I wanted some mashed potatoes with gravy and I said yes. She stuck a large bowl of the white and brown snack through the window to me. My dad also interupted to explain a part on why words were magic. Olden day magicians would know the essence of a word, and when they said it right, it would make things happen. Every time I was interupted, I resumed reading to my father. After the story was finished, my dad told me he thought it was good. He read some parts to himself, and he said the story rang true. I was a little

G. diappointed in that. I always expect better reactions from people, but he seemed not to think the story as important and beautiful as I believed.

H. The Door in the Air and Other Stories was such a true to life book. Changes of people and nature were illustrated with the enchanting fables of Margaret Mahy.

Following are Mimi's written and visual responses to the book *Others See Us*. On the entry slip for these pieces Mimi explained, "I chose to do a comic strip because the story was like a comic strip-type story: mind-reading, evil people, etc."

Response to Literature

High

Others See Us

A.   Reading *Others See Us*, by William Sleator, gave me a taste of what could happen if someone was able to look into other people's thoughts. The idea had frightening possibilities. The story told how some people used, and misused, the ability.

B.   The story was about Jared, who was visiting his Grandma's house and staying at a cottage with his parents on the 4th of July. At this time every year, his relatives would arrive to celebrate the 4th of July with a great picnic. This included Jared's cousin, sweet, beautiful Annelise, whom everyone loved and Jared hoped would become more than friends with that summer. But when Jared went on a bike ride and fell into a swamp, everything changed. The swamp was filled with toxic waste, and Jared found that somehow it gave him the power to read the thoughts and feelings of others. Jared learned how the power to read minds was linked with ATM robberies, houses going up for sale, and his and Annelise's journals being stolen. He soon found out that underneath, things are not always what they seem to be.

C.   At first, Jared hearing the thoughts of people around him gave me a headache because the peoples' many thoughts were confusing to listen to and read about. There were so many voices and Jared couldn't interpret them. But after a while, Jared learned to focus on only one person at a time, and things got very interesting. Using his mind-reading ability, he found out that Annelise was really a monster in disguise. She had a craving for attention and making sure that everyone loved her. She acted nice, caring, and friendly so people would think she was perfect. She was very pretty and everyone liked her. But on the inside she was not a shred bit beautiful. Annelise was conniving, mean, and would do anything for the love and attention of boys and everyone else. Jared, who had really liked Annelise, discovered the truth about her when her diary was stolen one morning and she thought of all the nasty paragraphs she had entered into it. Jared went into her mind and found out that Annelise liked having more than one boy at a time to get attention from and to have fun with. She even set up something that killed a girl who was going after her boyfriend. Annelise would do anything to keep up her sweet little image and get the attention from everybody. At first I couldn't believe that Annelise could act so sweet and be so cruel. But after Jared saw through her, it was like her image was ripped away and replaced by a terrible monster, black and ashy from her rotting personality. Through her looks and kind acts, Annelise was nothing more than that; a monster.

D.   I also couldn't imagine Jared's grandmother, spunky as she was, to have fallen into the swamp, too, and used her mind-reading ability to rob houses and ATM machines. She also blackmailed a disliked neighbor to sell their house and move away. When both Jared's and Annelise's journals were stolen, she told them that she was the thief and made them gather more swamp water in a jug for her unless they wanted their journals broadcast to their families. She knew that Annelise was really a terrible person since she could read minds, and she had developed a plan to have Annelise stopped from using and hurting people. She wanted to protect Jared and others from Annelise's nasty ways. But still, since Grandma misused her power, how well could she be trusted by anyone? If I was Jared, I would be glad her cleverness was working in favor of me, but Grandma's negative points would also make me unsure. The truth in people is probably best hidden, or else everybody would hate each other.

E.   I'm not really sure what I would do if I could read minds. Maybe I'd read the thoughts of someone I didn't really know or was curious about. Reading the thoughts of my friends or people that I thought disliked me could be risky. I'd feel like I was invading if I looked into my friends minds, and I wouldn't want to know how badly someone didn't like me. But for people I didn't really know, it would be fun to know their thoughts. I wouldn't have to face them, and I'd know secrets about them. It could probably help me understand people better. I could learn how a mind works. In a boring class I could just look around the room and read someone. I'd know the true feelings of someone despite their outer personality. I could also see how teachers really are. The possibilities are endless. Of course, I wouldn't want anybody to read my mind. My thoughts are my most private thing, and if anybody knew them, I'd be devestated. Sometimes I've thought about the possibility that someone could read my mind, and I just had to tell myself to forget the idea because it would be so terrible if it was true. But if I was the one to read minds, my motto would be *"What they don't know can't hurt them."*

F.   *Others See Us* was a great book that made me aware of the possibilities that mind-reading could bring. I found out that nobody is what people think. There's always the true thoughts that make up someone's inner personality. *Others See Us* had me speculating in suspense.

Rubric / Commentary

A. In the opening paragraph, the student engages the reader and previews book's content.

B. Effectively interweaves plot summary with personal response and interpretation.

C. Insightfully analyzes character.

D. Speculates about meaning of events.

E. Explores personal connections to literature.

F. Brings satisfying closure to piece.

Connections to Standards

Mimi demonstrates substantial achievement in:

• using written and visual language to communicate effectively (4);

• applying knowledge of language structure, language conventions, media techniques, and genre to create and critique print and nonprint texts (6).

Task

Students were asked to show responses to literature. Mimi used visual representation, in addition to her essay on *Others See Us.*

Rubric/Commentary

A. Skillfully translates plot and character into visual representations.
B. Controls conventions of comic strip action and dialogue.
C. Uses visual device to distinguish between characters' words and thoughts.
D. Ends appropriately for serial comic strip.

Task

Following is Mimi's reading record from late December to early June. She lists thirty-one entries, including science fiction and fantasy novels and short story collections. The works are challenging. Her teacher certified that Mimi had read and understood these books and wrote, "Her engagement is deep and her voice is always insightful and strong. She has read widely and thought deeply about concepts she finds in her reading."

High

Breadth of Reading

Rubric

The requirements for breadth in reading were:
at least twenty-five books (or equivalent);
a balance of literature and non-literary works;
at least three different genres or modes;
at least five different authors;
at least four books about one issue.

BOOK LIST

TITLE	AUTHOR	# PGS	STARTED	FINISHED	RATING 1 2 3 4 5 BEST 1 WORD DESCRIPTION	
THE SECRET GARDEN	FRANCES H. BURNETT	271	12-27-94	NEVER	3	A CLASSIC
THE PRINCESS BRIDE	ABRIDGED BY WILLIAM GOLDMAN	283	1-28-95	2-3-95	5	WONDERFULLY FUNNY, ADVENTURE
GRAVEN IMAGES	PAUL FLEISCHMAN	85	1-17-95	1-20-95	4	FUNNY & CHILLING
ANIMAL DREAMS	BARBARA KINGSOLVER	342	2-3-95	2-9-95	5	WONDERFUL!
TALES FROM THE SECRET ANNEX	ANNE FRANK	156	2-15-95	2-18-95	4	RELAXING, DIFFERENT
CHILDHOOD'S END	ARTHUR C. CLARKE	218	2-21-95	—	2	SLIGHTLY BORING, NOT FOR ME
THE BIGGER BOOK OF LYDIA	MARGARET WILLEY	215	3-1-95	3-2-95	5	RELATING, INTERESTING
THE GIVER	LOIS LOWRY	180	3-2-95	3-3-95	5	VERY DIFFERENT POINT OF VIEW
A CIRCLE UNBROKEN	SOLLACE HOTZE	202	3-3-95	3-5-95	5	MADE ME HAVE MIXED FEELINGS
THE LAST UNICORN	PETER S. BEAGLE	212	3-6-95	3-11-95	2½-3	PRETTY GOOD, BUT A STRANGE SORT OF NOVEL
TURTLE & OTHER STORIES MEAT	JOSEPH BRUCHAC	115	3-15-95	—	3	GOOD STORIES, BUT NOT ENOUGH TO HOLD ME
THE BEAN TREES	BARBARA KINGSOLVER	232	3-17-95	3-22-95	5	WONDERFUL GREAT DESCRIPTIONS, STORY!
NOT A SWAN	MICHELLE MAGORIAN	407	3-23-95	3-27-95	5	FUN EDUCATIONAL
KENTUCKY DAUGHTER	CAROL J. SCOTT	160	3-29-95	3-30-95	4½	RELATING, NICE
AMY'S EYES	RICHARD KENNEDY	437	3-31-95	4-2-95	5	GAVE ME A NEW VIEW OF DOLLS
PARDON ME YOU'RE STEPPING ON MY EYEBALL	PAUL ZINDEL	199	4-4-95	4-5-95	2½	ORDINARILY WEIRD
SHIZUKO'S DAUGHTER	KYOKO MORI	218	4-5-95	4-9-95	3¾	POINTS OF VIEW AT END BECAME VERY INTERESTING

Commentary

Very brief comments reflect engagement with reading.

Of the thirty-one entries, twenty-eight were completed between December 27, 1994, and June 14, 1995. This is a very good reading pace. Mimi is a fluent reader.

The list of books represents adequate breadth in voice, not genre.

The rankings (5 is tops) show what engaged the reader.

The organization of the list shows Mimi's skills at visual representation.

The list could have included the informational texts read for Mimi's research project (see page 76, Research Notes).

Connections to Standards

Mimi demonstrates substantial achievement in:

• reading a wide range of texts to build an understanding of texts, of herself, and of the cultures of the United States and the world (1);

• reading a wide range of literature (2).

The Magic Circle	Donna Jo Napoli	118	4-14-95	4-14-95	4	OFFERS TOUCHING EXPLANATION TO EVIL
Troubling A Star	Madeleine L'Engle	296	4-14-95	4-17-95	4½	LEARNED A LOT ABOUT ANTARCTICA INTERESTING
Where It Stops Nobody Knows	Amy Ehrlich	212	4-18-95	4-19-95	3¾	FUN TO READ ABOUT THE NEW PEOPLE & PLACES
Midnight Hour Encores	Bruce Brooks	263	4-19-95	4-20-95	2¼	MAIN CHARACTER/ NARRATOR WAS ARROGANT & EGOTISTICAL
Like Water For Chocolate	Laura Esquivel	241	4-21-95	4-22-95	5	A DELICIOUS WONDERFUL STORY. HARD TO PUT DOWN
Tiger Eyes	Judy Blume	222	4-22-95	4-24-95	4	LIKED READING ABOUT HER FEELINGS & THOUGHTS
Others See Us	William Sleator	163	4-27-95	4-28-95	5	A GREAT, SUSPENSFUL, THOUGHT-PROVOKING STORY
Rascal	Sterling North	189	5-5-95	5-10-95	3⁶⁄₇	RELAXING, BUT FELT BAD ABOUT KILLING OF THE ANIMALS
Shadow	Joyce Sweeney	216	5-11-95	5-11-95	3	SUSPENSE BUILT UP FOR SMALL INCEDENT. AUTHOR DIDN'T MAKE RIGHT POINT
Virtual Mode	Piers Anthony	323	5-12-95	5-20-95	4	I LIKED READING IT, BUT IT DIDN'T GIVE ME ANYTHING SPECIAL
The Door in the Air	Margaret Mahy	106	5-14-95	5-15-95	5	TRUE TO LIFE! ENJOYABLE & SHORT
California Blue	David Klass	199	5-20-95	5-22-95	4	ENVIRONMENTAL & HUMANISTIC BATTLE
Where I Want To Be	Cara DeVito	187	5-24-95	5-28-95	3¾	AT FIRST I DIDN'T LIKE THE MAIN CHARACTER, BUT THEN SHE WAS COOL
Wyrd Sisters	Terry Pratchett	252	6-3-95	6-14-95	5	FUNNY! I LOVED READING THIS LIGHT & COMIC STORY

Task

On the entry slip for this piece, Mimi explained that the assignment was to "write a poem that told what it's not telling." She continued, "I didn't exactly grasp the concept, but I still like the poem."

Cat

A.

*It is not me-- dancing
with the wind, crashing
out the door with the
wind blowing my hair
to the sky.*

B.

*It is not me--
reaching my hands toward
the wildly rocking trees
with a song in my head
and a step to my feet.*

C.

D.

*No, not me-- dancing and leaping
to the untamed blowing and moaning--*

*But my cat. With a jump
over the fence and a spark
in his eyes, bewildered
at the crazy girl who is
dancing with the wind.*

E.

F.

Rubric / Commentary

A. Establishes organizational pattern in first stanza.
B. Uses repetition (e.g., "dancing," "crashing," "reaching," "leaping") as a unifying device.
C. Creates striking visual images (e.g., "wildly rocking trees").
D. Uses sound devices (e.g., alliteration, assonance) effectively.
E. Final line echoes opening stanza.
F. Effectively creates mysterious mood.

Connections to Standards

Mimi demonstrates substantial achievement in:

• applying knowledge of language structure, language conventions, figurative language, and genre to create print texts (6).

Report of Information (Description)

On her entry slip, Mimi described the assignment as follows: "Everyone had to write about either a favorite author or research on a topic."

Rubric / Commentary

A. Factual opening paragraph clearly states thesis.

B. Used marginal graphic to indicate sections she had difficulty writing. Good visual representation.

C. Gives geographical context necessary for understanding animals' adaptation.

D. Organizes information by categories: marsupials, birds, reptiles, and amphibians.

E. Cites numerous details about marsupials. Good sense of evidence.

The Australian Desert Outback

A. Two thirds of the continent of Australia is the outback. One third of Australia is made up of deserts. The land is full of desert grasses, reptiles, birds, and marsupials. Being isolated on the island of Australia, many of the animals are unique and found nowhere else. Each plant and animal has adapted to the dry desert of the Australian outback.

B.

C. The outback, part of the dry interior, stretches across the country, from the Great Dividing Range in the east to the far western coastal rim. The Blue Mountains make up the Great Dividing Range, which blocks out the rain coming in from the Pacific Ocean. The deserts of the outback are made up of the Great Sandy Desert, Gibson Desert, Great Victoria Desert, and Nullarbor Plain. The average daytime temperature in the desert of the outback is 86 degrees Fahrenheit. The climate is dry and hot, with long periods of drought and occasional violent rainstorms and floods. The outback is dotted with occasional rivers and swamps. Eucalyptus trees are the main plants of the outback. Scrubby eucalyptuses, or short, stunted trees called mallees, are found in the dry interior. The ground is covered with a wide variety of sands, desert grasses, and brush. The driest desert area covered with gravel or loose stones is called a gibber.

HAD TROUBLE GATHERING INFORMATION ON THE GEOGRAPHY

D.

E. Many of the mammals are marsupials, animals that carry their young in a pouch. Kangaroos, wallabies, and koalas are the best known. Food is scarce in the desert of the outback; plants only flourish after the occasional rain. The animals have adapted to what they have. A honey possum is a marsupial that depends on nectar for its food. It has a long, slender, beak-like snout that fits inside flowers. A carnivorous marsupial, the mulgara, obtains water from the bodies of its prey. It never drinks. Koalas are about 2 feet high, with gray-brown fur and large furry ears. The females carry their young in a pouch on the rear. A koala looks like a gray teddy bear, but it is not. It is a marsupial that lives in the tops of eucalyptus trees. The koala has a diet of entirely eucalyptus leaves and gets all its liquid from them. The koala's name is the Aborigine word for "no water". The marsupials of the outback have adapted well to their environment.

F.

Most birds of the outback are honeyeaters. Many of the birds have long, thin beaks to drink nectar from tubular flowers. Though it doesn't eat nectar, Australia's largest bird, the emu, can run up to 45 miles per hour when being chased. The emu is a light, flightless bird with long legs. They have brown, coarse feathers and can reach a height of 6 feet. The large birds resemble ostriches and are the second largest bird in the world. The rainbow lorikeet has beautiful patches of blue, red, yellow, orange, green, and pink, and will breed after it rains. The budgerigar is one of the most popular pet birds in the world. There are many appealing birds in the outback.

G.

H.

Of these groups of animals, I think the reptiles and amphibians are the most interesting. There are a number of lizards in the outback, such as the knob-tailed gecko which washes its large eyes with its tongue. The frilled lizard may not seem like more than just a plain green lizard, but when it needs to scare off predators, it opens its mouth and expands the frill around its neck. The most interesting lizard is the moloch, or thorny devil. Though it's harmless, the brown and yellow lizard is studded with horns and spikes to keep away predators. Tiny grooves in it's skin pass along dew and water to its mouth to drink. Frogs in the outback mate only in wet conditions so their tadpoles can develop in pools of water and grow to be mature enough to not need water when the dry seasons come. Rivers and swamps contain small, freshwater crocodiles and large, dangerous estuarine crocodiles.

I.

Life in the Australian desert outback is dry and hot, but still, many unique and interesting plants and animals live there. Each life form has adapted and survived harmoniously to the climate, and is at home in the dry interior.

F. Establishes linkages between sentences (e.g., honeyeaters and emus).

G. Places probable topic sentence at end of paragraph, bringing some cohesion to a loosely knit collection.

H. Establishes linkages between paragraphs (i.e., "Of these groups of animals. . . .").

I. Overall structure unifies report.

Connections to Standards

Mimi demonstrates substantial achievement in:

● gathering, evaluating, and synthesizing data from a variety of sources to communicate her discoveries in ways that suit her purpose and audience (7);

● using a variety of informational resources to gather and synthesize information and to create and communicate knowledge (8).

T a s k

Mimi was asked to include research notes about her reading. Samples of Mimi's notes show that she consulted a variety of sources and selectively incorporated information read into her report.

Wildlife Fact·File

THE AUSTRALIAN. OUTBACK & ITS WILDLIFE
Group 10: World Habitats Card 3 4 pgs. including photos

This Wildlife Fact·File card told about the location, climate, & features of the Australian outback. It told the habits & special adaptions of the mammals, birds, reptiles, & amphibians.

KOALA
Group 1. Mammals Card 21 4 pgs including photos

This reference told the habitat, diet, breeding, & the relationship with man & koalas. Special features & lifestyle of the koala was told.

Australia   3-25

By Emily U. Lepthien Copyright © 1982
Regen steiner Publishing Enterprises, Inc.
Pgs. 9, 27, 28, 38, 45 - 70, 83, 84, 120

Tells history, geography, geology, industries, animals, Aboriginal, tourist attractions, & other information on Australia today.

REFERENCE 3 *Suprising Lands Down Under*
                                                      3-2

By Mary Ann Harrell - National Geographic Society
Copyright © 1989 The National geographic Society
Pgs. 66, 67, 72-74, 161, 186. & 187

Told about Australia & New Zealand. Gave facts & information on the culture, geography, & history of Australia especially, including information on the Aborigines, rain forests, **Great Barrier Reef**, the outback, wildlife, & cities.

On the entry slip, Mimi explained the assignment as follows: "Everyone was asked to write a narrative piece which would show how we planned, organized, revised, and the changes we made to improve our piece." Only excerpts of Mimi's final piece, her numerous drafts and planning activities are shown in the next few pages.

High

Writing in a Literary Genre: Fictional Narrative

Narrative Story *PROCESS PAPER*

Jovian Journal

A. *Day One* I was about to be changed into a Loper, the most intelligent life form from Jupiter. I had wanted something new, something different than Earth. I needed a change. On Earth, my life had no real meaning. I needed to find out who I was by going to Jupiter. So, that was why I was willing to leave. I was to be changed into a Loper to survive the surroundings. I was determined and ready to leave Earth forever.

B. I walked unexpectantly into the machine. It resembled a closet with a dial for the coordinates. The door shut closed. I waited in the chamber for ten minutes, soaking up the Loper knowledge that would change my physical and mental self. The silence pounded my ears, yet I learned so much from the deathly quiet. Slowly, I became a Loper.

C. My body wasn't fully developed, but I opened the door into Jupiter. The ammonia air tightened my human skin. I gasped as I breathed in the prickly vapors that collided into my heart and stopped it for seconds. I knew that my heart had changed. It was now dark blue and in the shape of a perfect circle. The air dryed

D. my eyeballs and I stood as a human statue until it rained. My mind saw the real Jupiter, not the one humans see. It was barren and beautiful with streaks of purple, blue, and another color only found in Jupiter that resembled the color of invisible suns. Then it rained. The ammonia drops that were clearish-yellow on Earth were turquoise-blue in Jupiter. They stained the brown

E. earth as they fell. Quickly, my skin melted and skimmed down my legs into a puddle. My clear nails shriveled and turned black as they dropped to the ground. My pink, raw skin burned to flames by the penetrating rain. An excruciating pain bolted throuugh my body as I burned. I moaned and screamed with human pain -- but,

R u b r i c / C o m m e n t a r y

A. Effectively introduces character and establishes setting.
B. Succinctly narrates first plot event.
C. Uses detail selectively.
D. Skillfully interweaves narration with description.
E. Chooses precise and vivid words, sometimes creating striking images (e.g. "my clear nails shriveled").

Paper continued on page 78

Fictional Narrative *(continued)*

F. Uses a variety of sensory details (e.g., sight, touch, smell).

G. Chooses precise and evocative words (e.g., "inched," "drenched," "intangible").

H. Creates effective scene from Durantee festival with many vivid details.

as I said, only human pain. As I slowly turned into a Loper, I accepted the pain and respected it as it took away something human from me. The fire burned away my worries and fears, or maybe gave me a new acceptance of them. The colors became brighter on Jupiter as my eyes took a new form.

Then, I saw them. Lopers slowly circled me. Their slug-like forms inched and slid around me. I had turned into a pile of black ashes, but was still alive. The Lopers made a sliding sound that I knew was now my call, my name. I rose out of the ashes, as

F. a Loper. My body was now a beige, smooth form resembling an Earth slug without the antennae. The black ashes of my human body became wet, and as I slid to my Lopers, I left a trail of black behind me. As they called me, I became sleepier and sleepier. The Lopers left me as I curled into a circle on the flat ground. I became drenched with silence — my sleep. I felt myself being covered with a lavender blanket that soaked me and let me smell a scent of lavender internally. I became replenished by the intan-

G. gible blanket and smelled it's aroma that comforted me. My mind went to a silent, quiet place as I fell asleep.

Day Two I awoke as a bright, white light rose into the sky. The light was a star that acted like an Earth sun. I was happy and replenished from my lavender blanket and I had no worries, fears, or felt depressed as I sometimes did before....

I soon learned that Jupiter was endless with life forms that were hiding, strange plants, and creatures. Jupiter was an infinate discovery. I followed a trail of spiky bushes along the brown ground until I found a village of light blue Durantees having a festival. They had giant, round bellies connected to two long, white crow-like legs and feet, and two light blue arms. Their faces were happy and cheerful with one eye and black lips

H. in a wavery upward turn. The Durantees greeted me with smiles and clicks of their tongue which was a respectful greeting for visitors. I called "Lowee!" which was my name, as a greeting. I watched them as they danced around a dark red and bright orange fire. They swayed their arms and moved their legs to the sound of their worshipped wind which blew and made music for them....

I. *Day Three* The next morning I found a lake. It was opaque purple and had little ripples circling in many places. I slid over a large boulder to see my reflection in the water. I looked over myself carefully. My two large eyes had downward curving eyelids and little green specks for my irises. I did look a lot like a slug, with smooth brownish-yellowish skin, but I also had little fishy scales on my sides. I moved my scales. They flapped outward like wings. Wings! In a rush of excitement, I fell head-first into the lake. It felt like my lavender blanket liquified. I made high-pitched noises as I struggled to get to the surface. Wriggling and writhing didn't get me anywhere but down faster, so I tried flapping my wings. It worked! My body was light and water-tight. A current of water was sent downward by my wings and I was pushed up high. And I didn't have to go up for air every few seconds like on Earth.

J. So I swam. I swam and swam and swam. It gave me an unbelievably free feeling. But then, I realized, I have always been free. Society has chained and cemented me to rules; or else I would have been an outcast, a weirdo. Here on Jupiter, there are no rules. We know things and we are enlightened. More than anyone on Earth could understand. And I swam. I finally knew who I was. Through the opaque purple, I am a Loper.

K.

I. Varies sentence structure and length.
J. Concludes by recalling theme of self-discovery.
K. Uses visual representation to engage readers.

Connections to Standards

Mimi demonstrates substantial achievement in:

• applying knowledge of language structure, language conventions, figurative language, and genre to create print and nonprint texts (6);

• using written and visual language to communicate effectively (4);

• employing a wide range of strategies as she writes and using different writing process elements appropriately (5);

• participating as a knowledgable, reflective, creative, and critical member of a literacy community (11).

Task

Students were asked to include evidence of the writing strategies used. To show her use of revision processes, Mimi includes drafts of her fictional narrative.

Final draft

This is the first paragraph of the final draft of the fictional narrative which is shown in its entirety on pages 77–79.

Narrative Story *PROCESS PAPER*

Jovian Journal

Day One I was about to be changed into a Loper, the most intelligent life form from Jupiter. I had wanted something new, something different than Earth. I needed a change. On Earth, my life had no real meaning. I needed to find out who I was by going to Jupiter. So, that was why I was willing to leave. I was to be changed into a Loper to survive the surroundings. I was determined and ready to leave Earth forever.

I walked unexpectantly into the machine. It resembled a closet with a dial for the coordinates. The door shut closed. I waited in the chamber for ten minutes, soaking up the Loper knowledge that would change my physical and mental self. The silence pounded my ears, yet I learned so much from the deathly quiet. Slowly, I became a Loper.

Draft 2

Draft 2 developed out of Mimi's meeting with a peer-editing group. Mimi's notes show her using writing to explore various revisions.

Rubric/Commentary

A. Drafts show the variety of strategies (colored pens, numbering) Mimi used to revise. Revisions are based on peer feedback.

B. Drafts show how Mimi revised to establish motivation of character and setting.

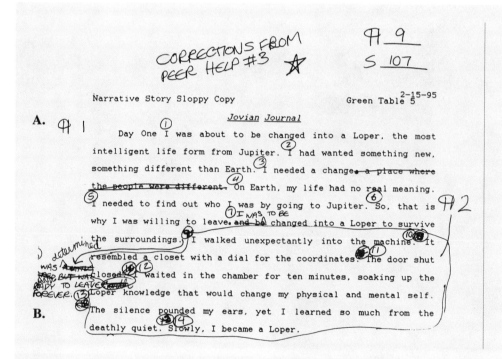

Task

Mimi met for a second time with her peer-editing group and collected notes once again based on the group's response (see next page). The teacher asked students to use a different-colored pen for each editing meeting. This change of pens allowed the teacher to trace changes over time in the narrative. Below is the draft following the meetings of the peer-editing group.

Rubric / Commentary

The student clearly marks the revisions from each meeting of the editing group.

MIMI'S PORTFOLIO

SENTENCES MADE IN RED PEN ARE AFTER 1ST PEER HELP.

CORRECTIONS MADE AFTER SECOND PEER HELP ARE IN BLUE PEN

Jovian Journal

I WANTED SOMETHING NEW, SOMETHING DIFFERENT THAN EARTH. I needed a change; a place where

Day One I was about to be changed into a Loper, the most intelligent *the best* life form from Jupiter. I walked *unexpectantly* into the machine. It resembled a closet with a *were* dial for the coordinates. I walked unexpectantly into the closet. The door shut *different* closed. I waited in the chamber for 10 minutes, soaking up the Loper knowledge *at so* that would change my physical and mental self. The silence pounded my ears, *was* yet I learned so much from the deathly quiet. Slowly, I became a Loper. *willing*

My body wasn't fully developed, but I opened the door into Jupiter. The *take* ammonia air tightened my human skin. I gasped as I breathed in the prickly *trip to* vapors that collided into my heart and stopped it for seconds. I knew that my *Jupiter* heart had changed. It was now dark blue and in the shape of a perfect circle. The air dried my eyeballs and I stood as a human statue until it rained. My *be changed* mind saw the real Jupiter, not the one humans see. It was barren and *into a* beautiful with streaks of purple, blue, and another color only found in Jupiter *Loper.* that resembled the color of invisible suns. Then it rained. The ammonia drops that were clearish-yellow on earth were turquoise-blue in Jupiter. They stained the brown earth as they fell. Quickly, my skin melted and skimmed down my *On Earth* legs into a puddle. My clear nails shriveled and turned black as they dropped to *my life had* the ground. My pink, raw skin burned to flames by the penetrating rain. An *no real* excruciating pain bolted through my body as I burned. I moaned and screamed *meaning* with human pain-- but, as I said, only human pain. As I slowly turned into a *I needed* Loper, I accepted the pain and loved it as it took away something human from *find out* me. The fire burned away my worries and fears, or maybe gave me a new *who I* acceptance of them. The colors became brighter on Jupiter as my eyes took a *was by* new form. *going to Jupiter.*

Task

Mimi's teacher provided a question/response form for peer-editing groups. By reviewing peer comments such as those below, Mimi began to identify problem areas to work on. Mimi included records of three peer conferences in her portfolio. Following is the record of her second peer conference. Note how Mimi eventually responded to her peer's suggestions.

A

Author_____
Evaluator_____

Date 2-14-95
Piece *Jovian Journal*

Questions for Peer Readers #2

1. How would you restate my position in a sentence or two.

You were tired and fed up with humans and Earth. You steped into some kind of transport that made you a Jovian and shipped you off to Jupiter where you encountered many adventures.

2. What other ideas can you offer to support my position?

You draw very well and I think an illustration could add a lot. Also I liked the way you separated the days. It made everything clearer and less confusing.

DREW → PICTURE

great advice and follow through!

3. What do you disagree with?

I think a better discription about what earth is like and how advanced we are would help and what time period does this take place. These all need some discription.

PUT IN SMALL SENTENCE WITH TIME PERIOD.

4. Where is my paper strongest or weakest?

It is strongest in realism and emotion. Because your emotions were expressed easily it seemed real. Not fictional or like a fairy tale. I liked it a lot. It reminded me of a book I read called "I spent my Summer Vocation in Outer Space."

Task

To help students begin developing the narrative, the teacher asked each student to try to develop a visual representation of a possible narrative. The chart (mind map) below was provided by the teacher to help students elaborate their narratives. Note that at the bottom right Mimi notes that she received peer assistance.

Rubric/Commentary

The student uses visual representation as a metacognitive tool for generating and organizing ideas. The student uses the representations that help, and leaves out others. (See next page also.)

MIND MAP 1

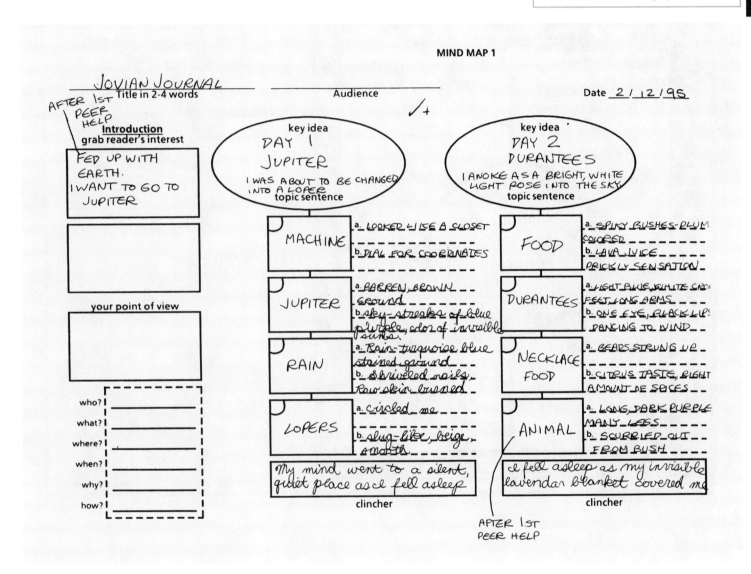

JOVIAN JOURNAL
Title in 2-4 words   Audience   Date 2/12/95

AFTER 1ST PEER HELP

Introduction
grab reader's interest

FED UP WITH EARTH.
I WANT TO GO TO JUPITER

your point of view

who?
what?
where?
when?
why?
how?

✓+

key idea
DAY 1
JUPITER
I WAS ABOUT TO BE CHANGED INTO A LOPER
topic sentence

MACHINE
a. LOOKER LIKE A CLOSET
b. DIAL FOR COORDINATES

JUPITER
a. BARREN, BROWN ground
b. sky–streaks of blue purple, color of invisible suns.

RAIN
a. Rain–turquoise blue stained ground
b. shriveled nails, raw skin burned

LOPERS
a. circled me
b. slug–like, beige, smooth

My mind went to a silent, quiet place as I fell asleep
clincher

key idea
DAY 2
DURANTEES
I AWOKE AS A BRIGHT, WHITE LIGHT ROSE INTO THE SKY
topic sentence

FOOD
a. SPIKY BUSHES–PLUM COLORED
b. LAVA JUICE PRICKLY SENSATION

DURANTEES
a. LIGHT BLUE, WHITE SKIN FEET, LONG ARMS
b. ONE EYE, BLACK LIPS DANCING TO WIND

NECKLACE FOOD
a. BEADS STRUNG UP
b. CITRUS TASTE, RIGHT AMOUNT OF SPICES

ANIMAL
a. LONG, DARK PURPLE MANY LEGS
b. SCURRIED OUT FROM BUSH

I fell asleep as my invisible lavender blanket covered me
clincher

AFTER 1ST PEER HELP

Task

The teacher gave Mimi a second visual representation to help her sort out the components of the narrative. In this procedure, the teacher has combined <u>knowing that</u> (what is a theme?) and <u>knowing how</u> (how are parts combined?).

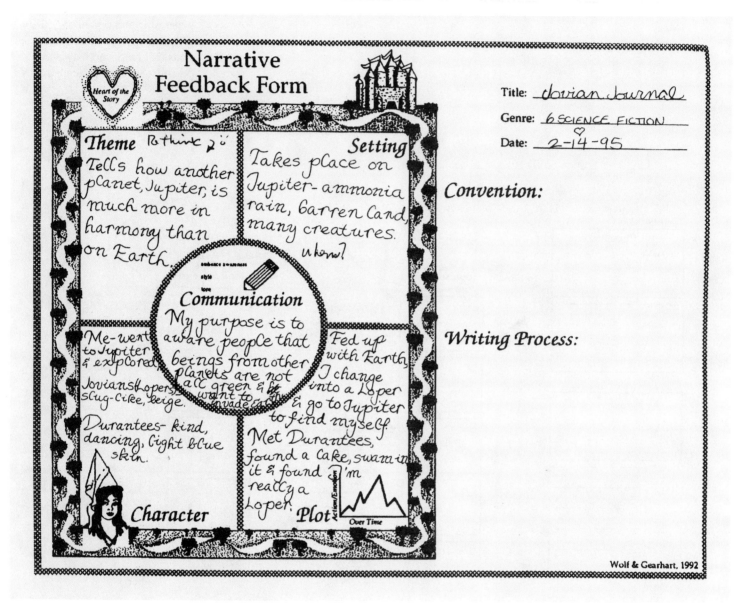

Summary Commentary of Mimi's Portfolio

Mimi's portfolio shows she has attained a substantial level of achievement in the English language arts. The artifacts presented suggest that Mimi has excellent encoding skills. In addition, her writing exhibits adequate mastery of conventions, such as spelling, usage, and punctuation. While some errors are noticeable, they are not distracting. In reading, the quantity and quality of the evidence presented (e.g., reading records, background reading for "The Australian Desert Outback," and book projects) suggest that Mimi is a fluent reader who comprehends a range of challenging literary and informational texts. One judge who scored Mimi's portfolio commented:

> ["The Door in the Air" shows] extreme complexity of thought and appreciation of ideas learned from the author.... [The student] takes an aesthetic stance in response to literature read...[and] critically questions texts.

The artifacts in Mimi's portfolio suggest that she is skilled at processing information and uses a variety of strategies to understand and to represent ideas. She sketches, outlines, seeks the advice of peers and others, drafts and redrafts. Her reflective essay and entry slips show that she is aware of her reading and writing processes, can set and achieve specific goals, and can articulate both strengths and weaknesses. Mimi's portfolio contains several examples of her ability to locate information, manipulate it, and translate it into other forms. For example, in her response to *Others See Us*, Mimi extracts from her reading salient themes and qualities of characters and translates them into a comic-strip format for an audience of peers. "The Australian Desert Outback," while not as engaging as other pieces in Mimi's portfolio, shows that she can select and effectively narrow a topic, formulate a stance toward it, and convey information efficiently and logically.

Mimi's writing reflects her skill at processing information and structuring texts. One judge who scored Mimi's portfolio commented that her writing "provides constant linkages through excellent introductions and conclusions, and excellent paragraph structure with topic sentences and clincher sentences."

The portfolio pieces show that Mimi writes for a range of close and distant audiences. This range of audiences includes her own reflective self ("Reading and Writing Self-Profile"), peers (e.g., "*Others See Us*," "Jovian Journal"), teachers, and other interested readers ("Australian Desert Outback," "Cat"). Likewise, her portfolio selections show that she writes skillfully about close (e.g., "*The Door in the Air and Other Stories*") and distant ("Australian Desert Outback") subjects.

Mimi writes in a variety of forms: reflective essay, response to literature, fictional narrative, report of information, poetry. Mimi also reads and responds to a broad range of materials, as her reading list and informational report suggest. Judges who scored Mimi's portfolio did note, however, that Mimi might expand her reading with more nonfiction works and a wider variety of fiction genres.

Mimi's portfolio selections show that she is conversant with key concepts in English such as theme, plot, character, setting, point of view (e.g., "*The Door in the Air and Other Stories*" and "*As Others See Us*"). In her responses to literature, she shows serious consideration of cultural ideas, such as the role of art in human existence and patterns of character, change and transformation. In the narrative "Jovian Journal," Mimi explores the idea of a search for meaning and the need for transformation.

Overall, Mimi's portfolio demonstrates that she has a high level of declarative knowledge (knowing that), which enables her to read and write fluently; procedural knowledge (knowing how), which enables her to read a broad range of texts and write in a variety of genres; and background knowledge (knowing about), which enables her to perform well in almost every task she has undertaken for this portfolio. Although a reader of Mimi's portfolio can easily perceive ways in which Mimi might improve her reading and writing even more (e.g., read more nonfiction works, use more complex sentences in writing, show evidence of persuasive writing), Mimi's work is unquestionably in the high range of performance.

Portfolios

Mimi

Reggie

Greg

Reggie compiled his portfolio at the end of his eighth-grade year. His portfolio represents a selection of the work he completed over the course of the school year. We have selected only a few pieces. Some of the pieces are excerpts only.

T a s k

Reggie chose to include a cover (below) with his portfolio.

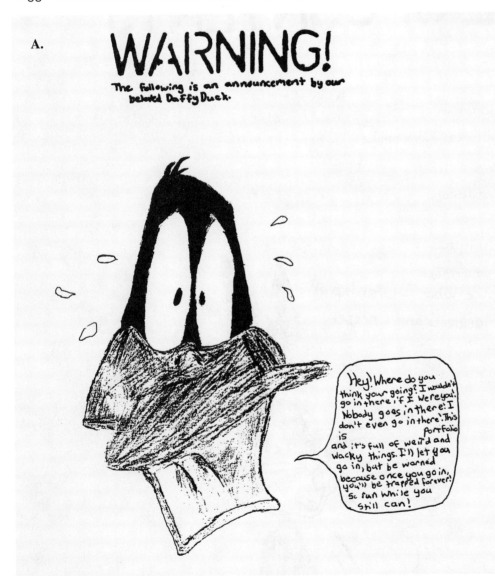

A.

R u b r i c / C o m m e n t a r y

A. The humorous and skillfully done cartoon and captions immediately engage the reader. Reggies uses the cartoon to add a "Let's have some fun" tone. The cartoon also allows Reggie to laugh about work for grades ("How many carrots am I getting?") and school life in general.
B. Effectively mimics language of Daffy Duck.

B. Do to temporary insanity, Daffy's message is not true and you should not listen to it. Although the weird and wacky things is the only true part to the message. So by all means. Please prepare yourself for a wild and wacky ride! Oh and have a nice day.

T a s k

Not all entries listed in Reggie's table of contents appear here. Reggie continues the cartoon theme with another artfully drawn character. In the humorous caption, Reggie plays with language and slyly (not so slyly?) hints at his understanding of the purpose of the portfolio ("how many carrots am I getting?").

TABLE OFCONTENTS

1. Letter of Introduction
2. Essay: One of the Great Compromises
3. Time of the Twins
4. Autumntime Conclusion
5. Reading Log
6. Propaganda Techniques
7. Script for Our Commercial
8. What I Want To Be When I Grow Up
9. How to Make Macaroni and Cheese

Task

The teacher asked students to open the portfolio with a letter or reflective essay introducing the portfolio and the patterns of its contents.

Letter of Introduction

A.   This is my letter of introduction. It plays an important part in my portfolia. This letter

B. sums up my progress in English class this year. This is possibly the most important writing in my portfolio. This piece of writing tells were I stood as a writer. This is were I evaluate my own work. Now as a writer I think this is one of the tuffest jobs because it's hard to judge your own work.

C.   Right now I think I stand as a strong and talented writer. I have my weak writings and I have my strong ones, but everyone does. Some examples of my strong writings are Script for our Commercial, Time of the Twins

D. (talking about a book), Journal Entry, and Propaganda Techniques. Out of these four I would have to say the Time of the Twins is my best. I have many other good writings, but these are just a few. The rest I would consider to be my weak ones.

   I really love writing. When I write stories I like to write ones that keep you in suspense. The genres that I use are

E. mystery, adventure, and horror. Horror is my personal favorite genre to use. In the summer time I usually write when I have nothing to do.

F. Sometimes I write for the heck of it.

REGGIE'S PORTFOLIO

Paper continued on page 90

G. Identifies general strengths and
weaknesses as listener and
speaker.

H. Identifies a general goal for
improving speaking but does not
name any specific strategies for
achieving it.

I. Provides general summary of
achievement in writing.

J. Directly addresses reader in
conclusion and invites reader's
feedback on his work.

K. Brings energy and caring to his
work.

Connections to Standards

Reggie is developing skill in:

• adjusting his use of written language to communicate effectively with a variety of audiences and for a variety of purposes (5).

G. Where I stand as a listener would be pretty good. I listen to all directions when given. I listen to the teachers when they are talking, I listen to pretty much everything. So I consider myself a good listener.

Now, as a speaker, I really stink at that. This is **H.** one of my worst qualities. I can't speak in front of a group in less if some of my friends are with me. When I'm by myself I get all nervous and start shaking. I have to work on this a lot or I won't do good in life, especially if I have to give a speech in front of a large group

I think my year in, two of the three, has gone really good, my writing especially. Sometimes I think that if I keep up my work as a writer **I.** that I will become a famous author. I hope someday I do because, like I said before, I love writing. I hope you have fun reading my portfolio and if I have any mistakes, I would like it if you would point them out for me, so that I can fix them **J.** when it returns. This will really encourage me to **K.** be the best writer that I can be!

Task

This assignment required the student to select an academic issue, to gather information about it, and to write an analytical essay on the subject.

Response to Informational Texts

Essay: One of the Great Compromises

A.   One of the compromises that was fought over at the Convention was over slave trade and navigation. At the Convention the South

B.   argued over the fact that they wanted no interference in its slave trade. While the North argued over the fact of navigation acts

C.   to be passed by a simple majority vote. The South, however, didn't like this idea and fought for a two-thirds majority vote. They also argued over the fact of export duties which the North favored while the South, opposed

D.   it. So then a compromise was worked out between the states. The states all agreed that there would be no interference with slave trade for twenty

E.   years. They also agreed to the navigation acts that they were to be passed by a simple majority vote and that there

F.   would be no federal taxes on exports.

G.   So as you can see that the compromise was worked and the states got what

H.   they wanted.

Rubric / Commentary

A. Clearly states topic.
B. Demonstrates understanding of information read about historical event.
C. Clearly describes opposing positions and nature of compromise.
D. Demonstrates understanding of the concept of "compromise."
E. Does not analyze, interpret, or evaluate information read.
F. Awkward phrasing here and there.
G. Does not make personal connections or connections to anything outside the text.
H. This assignment could be identified as a report of information (comparison/contrast: North vs. South).

Connections to Standards

Reggie is developing skill in:

• reading to acquire new information (1).

Response to Literature (Evaluation)

Task

Students were asked to include evidence of their response to literature. On the entry slip for this piece Reggie wrote, "I think it is one of my stronger pieces and feel that teachers would like it. This piece had no mistakes."

Rubric / Commentary

A. Opens abruptly without setting context for readers.

B. Identifies central moment in text, but does not provide sufficient context for event.

C. Provides general justification for retelling this portion of the plot.

D. Advances critical judgment about why the book appeals to young people.

E. Makes strong personal connections to events in text.

Time of the Twins
by Margaret Weis & Tracy Hickman

April 27, 1995

A. The most exciting event in the book was toward the end. Toward the end of the book jumped into the Cataclysm. The Cataclysm is a war when the gods were mad at the people of Istar and drop a mountain on the whole town. Before the Cataclysm started the gods sent warnings to the people by earthquakes, cyclones, storms, floods, and deaths. During the Cataclysm the High Tower started to fall apart (on the final earthquake)

B. and Tas (a main character) got caught under part of the roof that was falling and was knocked into the Abyss. The Abyss is a different plain. Then Caramon and Raistlin time traveled further ahead in time and get stuck there. I guess why this part is exciting

C. is because it's cool to see what happens to some characters that you never thought would happen to them.

What makes this book appealing to people my age is that it puts you in another reality. This book makes fantasies happen that people thought couldn't happen.

D. It brings out your wildest dreams of other worlds, people, races, and creatures that have never existed. It makes you want to jump into the book and

and become part of that reality. It would be cool to people our age to become a mighty warrior or

E. a wild and crazy mage (magic-user). To learn things that are impossible for us to learn. To experience the unexperienced. To dream the unimaginable dreams. To live the lives of some truly awesome characters. It's like opening up a new world in your very eyes and minds. That's why it would be appealing to kids

F. my age I believe this book will be popular in thirty years because the Dragonlance titles are doing much more great work and people would want to buy all the titles to find out what happens next.

G. From one cliff hanger to the next. Dragonlance books will be the best from years to come.

Connections to Standards

Reggie is developing skill in:

● evaluating and appreciating texts (3).

Middle

Task

After reading the short story "Autumntime," Reggie wrote the following conclusion to it.

Response to Literature (Fictional Narrative)

Autumntime Conclusion

A. When I got home I was still fingering the object that I had picked up in O'Briens backyard. I found the object so spellbinding, that I couldn't stop looking at it. I asked mom if it was an acorn but she didn't know neither did dad So I decided to get information on it at the West Boston Learning Center 4.

B. I took the elevator bus up to the fourth level, were I got on the same air track that we had took to Brooklyn. I got off at the stop and took another elevator bus to the main level. I then took the monorail to the Intercity Subway

C. Station 27 and got on the second sublevel AA train back to Boston.

D. I finally got to main Boston (again), rode the elevator-bus to ground level and took an air cush taxi to the Boston Learning Center 4. When I got to the Learning Center 4 I hopped out of the cab and took off to the stairs and climbed them with ease. When I reached the doors they opened up automatically and I walked in. Then a voice came over a loud speaker and welcomed me to the Learning center 4.

E. Then the voice asked where I wanted to go, I told it to take me to the section about trees of the old

F. The voice came back on and said thank you, and have a nice day and then shut off. I started to walk to the destination but the floor moved on me. So I just let the floor take me where I wanted to go.

Rubric/Commentary

A. Shows understanding of text read by extending it appropriately.

B. Maintains first-person perspective.

C. Loses momentum through inclusion of too many details of journey.

D. Recounts journey to Boston with coherence and concrete detail.

E. Uses some variety in transitions but overuses "then."

F. Makes occasional errors in sentence structure.

Paper continued on page 94

G. Effectively concludes incident.

A voice came on and told me that acorns can be buried to make a tree. Thats all I wanted to hear and took off running down the hall. By the time I took all the rides back home, it was late. But that didn't stop me. I went straight to mom and dad and asked them if there was any place to bury this. They both talked it over and said no there wasn't

G. I was sad but I didn't throw the acorn away. I just put it in my safe and kept it as a souvenir of the old world.

Connections to Standards

Reggie is developing skill in:
• applying knowledge of genre to create print texts (6).

Middle

Breadth of Reading

Task

Following is Reggie's reading record. Reggie's teacher wrote, "This portfolio demonstrates real learning.... [Reggie] does give evidence of making connections, [reading] a wide variety of literature, new interpretations of text, and evidence of growth."

Rubric

The requirements for breadth of reading were:
at least twenty-five books (or equivalent);
a balance of literature and non-literary public discourse;
at least three different genres or modes;
at least five different authors;
at least four books about one issue.

Commentary

The student did not document reading ten books in one semester. Thus, the student fell below the minimum expectation.
The ratings suggest that the student could have distinguished among responses and maybe did not.

Connections to Standards

Reggie is developing skill in:
• reading a wide range of literature and nonfiction (1, 2).

Literature   Reading Requirements

This year I will be requiring you to read at <u>least</u> 10 books during this first semester. I am requiring that you experience different genres each semester. This assignment will be worth 3 grades in the grade book, so it would be very beneficial to keep this sheet and accurate records of what you have read. If you should lose it, please ask for another one before it is due; you will be given 3 0's if you fail to turn it in. Record the following:

Genre	Name of the Book	Author	Date Completed	Rating
Teen Award	The Shadow Brothers	A.E. Cannon	10-7-94	10
Non-fiction				
Sports	Barry Bonds	Harvey Miles	11-30-94	10
Informational	Sports Great: Cal Ripken Jr	Glen MacNow	12-4-94	10
Science Fiction	Pet Sematary	Stephen King	9-28-94	10
Fantasy	Dealing with Dragons	Patricia C.Wrede	11-14-94	10
Realistic Fiction (mystery)	The Other Side of Dark	Joan Lowery Nixon	10-19-94	10
Realistic Fiction	On the Far Side of the Mountain	Jean Craighead George	9-2-94	10
Realistic Fiction	Call of the Wild	Jack London	12-25-94	10
Realistic Fiction				

This entry includes, first, Reggie's written report on the propaganda techniques of advertising; second, drafts and planning of the final report; and, third, the script for a commercial presented to his class.

Propaganda Techniques

Propaganda Techniques are what commercial artists use to convince people to go out and buy a product. These techniques have been used for many years and still are being used today There are eight different kinds of techniques that are used but I will be explaining them later. Propaganda Techniques have been successful for quite sometime. From my point of view propaganda techniques have affected kids, teens and adults. Propaganda Techniques will be around for millions of years.

Testimonial is one of the oldest techniques used today Testimonial is when a famous person endorses the product. One of these people is Micheal Jordan. Jordan endorses many companies, a few he endorses are Nike, Hanes, and Wheaties. There are many people out in the world who think that if they buy the product, they would be exactly like the famous person. This one really works on people.

"Cadillac Style" would be part of this next technique called Snob Appeal. Snob Appeal gives you the idea that the product is the best. Hallmark uses the phrase "Care to Give the Very Best" to make you believe that Hallmark's cards are the best you can buy. Most of the time the product that uses snob appeal ends up costing to much and is usually a piece of junk. So when people receive cards or whatever they check to see if it is a Hallmark card or the best product that you can find.

Whenever you see a commercial on t.v. where everybody is doing one thing then that is called Bandwagon. Bandwagon is when the commercial is trying to say join the crowd Pepsi and Dr. Pepper are a couple of companies that use bandwagon. Pepsi has it's "Pepsi Generation" and Dr. Pepper has "Be a Pepper" You also

Rubric / Commentary

A. Clearly defines term, "propaganda techniques."
B. Previews content of paper (explaining eight kinds of techniques).
C. Good thesis sentence, expressing personal opinion about topic.
D. Weakly indicates position toward topic.
E. Uses numerous specific examples to demonstrate understanding of terms.
F. Shows attention to audience by selecting widely recognized examples.
G. Concludes each paragraph with statement of personal opinion, thereby clarifying the direction of the description.

A.

B.

C.

D.

E.

F.

G.

Paper continued on page 96

H. Each paragraph explains a different technique but techniques are not prioritized or otherwise organized.
I. Effectively varies paragraph beginnings.
J. Exhibits some confusion about technique called "glittering generalities."
K. Uses transition words (e.g., "final") appropriately.
L. Brief but engaging conclusion.
M. Addresses reader directly throughout piece.
N. Does not provide documentation of source of information.
O. The student shows an adequate sense of simple sentence structure and an adequate command of the basic conventions of punctuation, spelling, capitalization, and so forth. There are some errors, but these errors create awkward moments, not damaging confusions.

Connections to Standards

Reggie is developing skill in:

• gathering, evaluating, and synthesizing data (7);

• communicating his discoveries in ways that suit his purpose and audience (7).

see commercials where everyone is smoking or drinking beer. These are all bandwagon commercials and they should be ignored.

H. When people use words to make you buy it is called Glittering Generalities. Some commercials use this technique, but not all of them do. A couple of examples are "Get Vertical" used by Mountain Dew and "Like a Rock" used by Cheurolet. These commercials don't always work on people except; the Mountain Dew commercials.

I. Uncle Ben's Rice would be an example of this next technique called Plain Folks Plain Folks is when they use ordinary people to sell things. There are many foods out on the shelf that uses ordinary people's names to sell them, a few of these are Mrs. Applebee's pie and Uncle Ben's Rice which I already

J. mentioned. You might even have someone in your family that is sloppy and you call him Sloppy Joe. One more example would be the   Lottery. On these commercials they usually have a family up there holding a big check saying a bunch of junk and crying. All of these are examples of plain Folks.

The technique that mixes facts, opinions, and that missleads is called Astortion. Two examples would be loss leaders and record clubs. Record clubs are the best at distortion. They tell you that you can buy 10 cd's, tapes, or records for a penny and after you buy them they send you a big bill and an order form for more. Distortion can really make people buy.

K. The final technique is called Name Calling.

L. Name Calling has the other product in the ad with them. Pepsi vs. Coke is always a common Name Calling you see on tv. Burger King vs. McDonalds and MCI vs. AT+T are now using Name Calling in their

M. commercials. These ads try to get you to change your drink, burger, or whatever to the one on the ad These sometimes work.

N.

O. So that is propaganda techniques and how they work. Don't buy into them.

Uncle Ben's Rice would be an example of this next technique called Plain Folks. Plain Folks is when they use ordinary people to sell things. There are many foods out on the shelf that uses ordinary people's names to sell them, a few of these are Mrs. Applebee's pie and Uncle Ben's Rice which I already mentioned. You might even have someone in your family that is sloppy and you call him Sloppy Joe. One more example would be the Lottery. On these commercials they usually have a family up there holding a big check saying a bunch of junk and crying. All of these are examples of plain Folks.

Final Draft

Final draft of "Uncle Ben's" paragraph. Selected paragraph shown on page 96.

Uncle Ben's Rice would be an example of this next technique called Plain Folks. Plain Folks is when they use ordinary people to sell thing. There are many foods out on the shelf that uses ordinary people's names to sell them, a few of these are Aunt (Jamima) Syrup and Uncle Ben's Rice which I already mentioned. You might even have someone in your family that is sloppy and you call him Sloppy Joe. One more example would be the Lottery. On these commercials they usually have a family up there holding a big check saying a bunch of junk and crying. All of these are examples of Plain Folks.

Earlier Draft

An earlier draft of the "Uncle Ben's" paragraph is shown here along with the final version above. Aware that he had spelled "Jemima" incorrectly, Reggie solved the problem by substituting "Mrs. Applebee's pie."

C o n n e c t i o n s
t o   S t a n d a r d s

Reggie needs to show substantial improvement in:

• employing a wide range of strategies as he writes (5);

• using different writing processes appropriately (5).

Task

The assignment asked students to preplan the report of information. The outline was suggested as one way to preplan.

Propaganda Techniques

I. Testimonial - famous person endorses product
  A. Micheal Jordan
  B.
    1. Nike
    2. Wheaties
    3. Hanes
    4. Gatorade
    5. McDonalds
  B. Nancy Kerrigan
    1. Campbells soup
    2. Disneyland
    3. Reebok

II. Snob Appeal
  A. Cadillac Style
  B. Hallmark "Care to Give the Very Best"

III. Bandwagon - join the crowd
  A. Dr. Pepper
  B. Pepsi Generation
  C. QVC

IV. Transfer - pictures to convey messages - emotion
  A. Girls in truck ads
  B. Pizza Hut
  C. Cola in ice

V. Glittering Generalities - uses words to make you buy
  A. Get Vertical
  B. Like a rock

VI. Plain Folks - uses ordinary people
  A. Uncle Ben's
  B. State Farm "Like a Good Neighbor"
  C.   Lottery

VII. Distortion - mixes facts and opinions, missleads
  A. Loss Leader
  B. Record Clubs

VIII. Name Calling - has the other product in the ad with them
  A. Pepsi vs. Coke
  B. McDonalds vs. Burger King
  C. MCI vs. AT+T

Task

In reports of information, students were asked first to learn declarative knowledge about their subjects (<u>knowing that</u>). Reggie presented this information in his research notes (outline) and report of information. This script assignment asked students to apply (<u>knowing how</u>) their declarative knowledge about propaganda by writing an advertisement.

A.

Script for our commercial

In our first hour English class we have just finished a unit on Propaganda Techniques. Propaganda Techniques are what commercial artists and companies use to try and get you to buy their product. After learning about these techniques we thought we would put them to use and make our own commercials.

When we got in our groups we had to come up with our own product and slogan. We came up with the idea of the Late Date Dating Service. Our slogan was "For those who only get out in the dead of the night." Our commercial consisted of four parts: 1. The Announcer 2. The Woman 3. Nerd #1 and 4. Nerd #2. We did our commercial on tape and had Tal + Eric lip the parts of the two nerds in front of the camera during filming. Aaron did the announcer's voice + both nerds on the tape and his cousin did the woman's voice. Here's how our script went.

B.

Announcer: "Work the swing shift? Can't get out until real late? Then call Late Date at 1-800-LAT-DATE and find the right mate."

Woman: "Call Late Date. For those who only get out in the dead of the night."

Nerd #1: "My love life used to take the graveyard shift until I called Late Date."

Woman: "Call Late Date."

Nerd #2: "I thought it was to late for me until I found out about Late Date."

Woman: "Call now."

Announcer: "That's 1-800-LAT-DATE."

C.

The technique used for our commercial was called Transfer. The reason we made this product and thought that people would use it is because we thought it was a pretty cool idea and most people don't get out until real late to date anyway, so we thought that it was pretty sufficient. The people that I worked with on this commercial were

What I learned on this was how to make a commercial and a good product that we can sell. I also learned the secrets that commercial artists use to sell a product. I thought that this was a fun experience and I think next years eigth graders should do this same project. I will be surprised if I hear some of them say that this wasn't fun because I thought it was worth it.

D.

Rubric / Commentary

A. Clearly explains assignment and group process.
B. Uses conventions of script-writing.
C. Applies understanding of propaganda techniques to original product (dating service).
D. Assesses own learning.

Connections to Standards

Reggie is developing skill in:

• applying knowledge of media techniques to create print and nonprint texts (6).

99

Reflective Essay

Reggie included this piece in his portfolio as a "Free Pick." He selected it "because it brings out an idea that I wanted to share with people."

Rubric/ Commentary

A. Clearly states topic but digresses almost immediately.
B. Recounts personal experiences related to topic.
C. Explains role of education in prospective career and speculates about probable requirements of job.
D. Ends abruptly and introduces new topic.

Connections to Standards

Reggie is developing skill in:

• using written language to accomplish his own purposes (12).

What I want to be when I grow up

Today I'm writing about what I want to be when I grow up.

A. When I grow up I plan on being a vet full time. I think being a vet is a cool job because you save peoples pets. Unlike some people who beat their pets and starves them to death. Some people are cruel and some are nice to animals. Saving animals is a cool job to do because you get to know the people and their pets. The reason why

B. I want to be a vet is because I had a friend who's dog was hit by a car and died instantly. The driver kept going and was never caught. You could tell the guy was drunk. I also had a bird die in my hands because it had snapped it's neck. I was going to take it to the vet but it died in fifteen minutes. I don't like killing animals because it's cruel. But if they were rabid then I would let people put them to sleep.

I am planning to go to college to get my degree to be a vet. It takes about two years to get your degree.

C. I would probably take classes in science and math because thats what you would need take. You would need to take these classes because you need to know what medicines to use and you probably need to add up like the ounces of drugs to use and the persons bill. So thats what I want to be when I grow up.

D. But if I couldn't be a vet I would want to be a cartoonist or a comedian.

Task

Reggie was asked to write directions for a procedure (cooking, fixing something, walking to the park). This kind of task requires the writer to keep the needs of the reader in mind and not to miss any crucial steps. On the entry slip, Reggie explained that he chose this piece because "it explains how to do something and I thought people could learn from this piece. If they don't know how to do it which I doubt."

Narrative (Explaining a Procedure)

Middle

How to Make Macaroni & Cheese

The first step in making macaroni.. from a box is to retreive it from your cupboard. Then you get out a pan and fill it full of hot or cold water and place on a burner on the stove. Then get your box of macaroni, open it, and take the cheese packet out and put it on the table. Next pour the noodles in the pan of water and turn on the burner underneath it. To on the timer for 15 minutes until noodles are cooked. So at this point you can watch t.v. or do something until the timer goes off.

Ok the timer went off so get up and head for the kitchen. Turn off the burner under the pan and check to see if your noodles are cooked. If they are get out the strainer and pour noodles into it until the water runs all out of them, then dump them back in the pan and put it back on the stove. Procede to the refrigerator and get out some milk and butter. Open up the pack of chesse and dump it in the pan. The take two spoonfuls of butter and dump that in too. Then pour in a little milk, but not to much. Turn on the burner again and stir the ingredents together. When it is all mixed together turn of burner and prepare to eat it.

When finished eating if any left over either store it for later or throw it away. Then be nice and do the dishes for your family. And then watch t.v. or something. And that's how you make macaroni and cheese.

A.
B.
C.
D.
E.

Rubric/Commentary

A. Conveys a set of directions in logical order.

B. Creates a humorous tone with use of asides ("So at this point you can watch t.v. . . . ." "Then be nice and do the dishes for your family").

C. Chooses direct, economical, and appropriate words for audience of peers.

D. Generates noticeable errors in spelling, punctuation, and pronoun reference. Errors do not seriously undermine communication, but they are a distraction which needs to be eliminated.

E. Uses concluding sentence.

Connections to Standards

Reggie is developing skill in:

• applying knowledge of language structure, language conventions, and genre to creat print texts (6).

Visual Representation

The final page of Reggie's portfolio provides an appropriate and light-hearted closure to his work.

Connections to Standards

Reggie is developing skill in:

• using written and visual language to accomplish his own purposes (12).

Summary Commentary of Reggie's Portfolio

The entries in Reggie's portfolio suggest that he is making progress toward reaching adequate levels of achievement in the English language arts. Reggie is developing encoding skills. Errors in spelling, punctuation, and usage are noticeable throughout the portfolio. Although somewhat distracting, the errors do not usually cause confusion about meaning. Reggie's writing is, for the most part, fluent, but he is still developing an "academic" style. In "Propaganda Techniques," for example, Reggie uses conversational expressions (e.g., "Most of the time the product that uses snob appeal…is usually a piece of junk. So when people receive cards or whatever they check to see if it is a Hallmark card.…"), and it appears he is still trying to learn how to write in academic contexts. Bibliographic citations, for example, do not appear in Reggie's research notes. Reggie's reading records and responses to texts (e.g., "Time of the Twins") show that he is a fluent reader who comprehends the gist of what he reads and who makes some attempts at interpretation.

The artifacts in Reggie's portfolio suggest that he is developing skill in processing information but uses a limited repertoire of strategies for understanding and representing ideas. The excerpt of the draft for "Propaganda Techniques" shows only one minor editorial change. While his outline for this paper shows that Reggie is competent in this method of planning for writing, he has included no other evidence of other strategies he uses in writing. Nor does he mention specific strategies or processes in his letter of introduction to the portfolio. Reggie's portfolio contains several examples of his ability to locate and use information, but he is not yet a skilled manipulator of informational texts. Since he did not document any reading (bibliographies) for "Propaganda Techniques" or "Essay: One of the Great Compromises," it is difficult to determine whether he can identify, select, and synthesize information gained from reading. Reggie's responses to literature ("Time of the Twins," "Autumntime Conclusion") show that he is beginning to develop interpretations, but that he does not yet analyze, critique, or evaluate the texts he reads. He makes personal connections to texts, but does not make connections to larger ideas or issues.

Reggie has an engaging, well-developed personal voice, but he has not provided evidence that he can write for a range of audiences. The cover, table of contents, and final page of Reggie's portfolio are clearly intended to engage readers of his portfolio, as is the final paragraph of his letter of introduction. But all the pieces in Reggie's portfolio share a similar conversational tone; his voice, though often charming, does not vary overall.

Reggie's portfolio pieces show that he is developing control of some forms of writing, e.g., report of information and explanation of procedure. He is beginning to experiment with literary forms ("Autumntime Conclusion") and has written a coherent response to literature ("Time of the Twins"). It would be interesting to see examples of some of the genres Reggie says in his letter of introduction that he enjoys writing: mystery, adventure, and horror. Reggie's reading evidence suggests that he is a competent reader who needs to read more and to develop his analytical, critical, and evaluative skills. His reading records portray a student who enjoys reading but rarely tackles challenging literary or informational texts.

The selections in Reggie's portfolio show that he understands some key concepts in English. For example, he identifies a main character in "Time of the Twins," and he maintains a point of view in "Autumntime Conclusion." While Reggie occasionally demonstrates some awareness of cultural ideas (e.g., the need for fantasy as shown in "Time of the Twins"), he does not grapple with them. For example, he does not explore the idea of "compromise" in the piece "One of the Great Compromises." Likewise, in "Propaganda Techniques," Reggie never goes beyond defining terms and giving examples.

Overall, Reggie's portfolio demonstrates that he has a high level of declarative knowledge (knowing that), but that he is still learning how to put that knowledge to use (knowing how). For example, Reggie knows that paragraphs and papers should have conclusions, but he has not yet mastered the skill of writing effective conclusions (e.g., "So as you can see that the compromise was worked and the states got what they wanted." "So that is propaganda techniques and how they work." "And that's how you make macaroni and cheese."). Although he does successfully adopt the voice of the protagonist in "Autumntime Conclusion," the personal voice of Reggie himself dominates the work in the portfolio. He does not provide evidence of knowing about other voices which speak to other audiences. Although he almost met the teacher's criteria for reading for the semester, Reggie's reading lacks breadth. In addition, he has provided no evidence that he has read in depth on any subject or concentrated his reading on any author or genre. Reggie's portfolio places his work in the middle range of performance. It provides a strong foundation from which to expand his repertoire of skills, strategies, and ideas.

Portfolios

Mimi

Reggie

Greg

Greg compiled this portfolio at the end of his seventh-grade year. His portfolio represents a selection of the work he completed over the course of the school year. We have selected only some pieces from Greg's portfolio to show you here.

Introduction

Task

The first task in Greg's portfolio is the letter of introduction.

Letter of introduction

Dear Reader,

I think I'm a pretty good reader writer and a language user because I try good at those things. My strengths are that I read more and write more. I would like to improve my reading. My goals are that I improve in anything I do. My special accomplishments is to get in education.

Well at home I dont write that much and I dont read that much but I do alot of stuff that has do to with language. at school I use these things every day.

Rubric / Commentary

In this sparse letter of introduction, Greg makes very vague statements about his strengths and goals.

He makes a connection between reading and writing in and out of school, but does not explore the meaning of this.

Noticeable errors in conventions occur here and there and continue throughout the portfolio.

Argument (Problem Solution)

Task

The assignment called for an argument, including a letter to the editor, focusing on an issue.

Letter TO Editor

A.
B. Dear Editor why are Pogs so Popular all around the world did yall know They were called milk caps and the first country that statered Playing Pogs was Hawiin. I think
C. Pogs are epicd because all they are is cardboard but why are the so Popular. My brother has
D. 4,000 Pogs and he is only 9 and he is really
E. good at Pogs I never Played Pogs and why are
F. Pogs illegal in school I think that is stupid.

Rubric / Commentary

A. Does not observe conventions of formal letter writing.
B. Begins as an argumentative essay or problem solution in the form of a letter to the editor, but the controversy is unclear.
C. Digresses by explaining background on pogs, brother's collection of pogs, and own experience with pogs.
D. Hints at true purpose in final sentence.
E. Mentions stance toward topic ("I think that is stupid.")
F. The writing shows some fluency.

Response to Literature

Task

The assignment called for a response to literature. This question/answer exercise was the only response to literature Greg included in his portfolio.

Rubric / Commentary

A. Identifies main character but does not explain why she is important.

B. Supports choice of Abigail as main character with a logical reason.

C. Demonstrates some understanding of character change.

D. States opinion about plot events.

E. Suggests plausible alternative endings for story.

Connections to Standards

Greg needs to show substantial improvement in:

• applying a wide range of strategies to comprehend, interpret, evaluate, and appreciate texts (3).

WEST AGAINST THE WIND

1. Choose one character in West Against the Wind. Why is this character important to the story?
A. abigal— she is the mean character in west agaisnt the wind, also she is in the book the most and
B. she wants to live with her dad

2. Did any character change? How did this character change? "will" changed alot because he never liked matteu because matteu had
C. something going on with abigal—and now will likes him because matteu said "will" live.

3. Describe, in detail, your favorite part of the story.
my favorite part was the boxt part when there was a fight.

4. What did you dislike about the way the author wrote the story.
i didike the part when abigal painted the wagon and
D. every body was made at her, so her dad can reconise them

5. How else might the author have ended the story?
he could of ened the story by will.. and matteu seater
E. fell in love and matteu and abigal get maried and abigal Dad could of strek rict in the gold mine

---

Task

The student was asked to write an imaginative story.

"The Kids with the revolver"

A. One day Kris, Jason, Nate Dogg, Paul, and Warren G were at Kris's house and Warran G house there mom was at work and it was summer. So Kris called his friend named Paul and Paul came over to warran G

B. called some of his friends to come over and Jason, Nate Dogg and warran were messing around in warran bedroom and they all decided to tate a walk. Kris and Paul they were going to play sega and mess around so when warren G and his friend came back they didn't notice that Kris and Paul were gone so Jason went into the kitchen to get some beer and it was all gone. One hour later Kris and Paul showed up and they were drunk and warran

C. came into Kris room and said are you drunk again if you are dm going to hit you so hard you will never wake up. Kris said no we were not drinking. So warran Jason and Nate Dogg were rapping in warran room. They were singing this d.J be warran

D. G and they heard a gun fire go off and warran Nate Dogg and Jason waleld right into Kris room and seen Kris on the floor and warran said called the cops and they did and warran looked at Paul and said what happend to my brother and Paul said we found a revolver and we didn't

E. know it was loded and he Pulled the triger and it fired. 2 Days later Kris is in the Hospital and warran G is

F. famous from rapping and his songs are the best thats what every body is saying. Kris in a comma and he want wake up intell a week maybe. The next day Kris is awatend in his home and

G. every body is happy

Rubric / Commentary

A. Names main characters and identifies setting.
B. Comings and goings of characters become confusing.
C. Uses dialogue, but does not observe conventions of punctuation.
D. Long series of events joined by "and's."
E. Abrupt shifts in action and scene without explanation or motivation (e.g., Warren G is famous for rapping; Kris wakes up from coma).
F. Spelling errors cause confusion about meaning.
G. Demonstrates rudimentary understanding of plot.

Connections to Standards

Greg needs to show substantial improvement in:

• applying knowledge of language conventions and genre to create print texts (6).

GREG'S PORTFOLIO

Breadth of Reading

The teacher asked each student to keep a reading record showing at least the minimum requirements (see below).

Rubric

The student was asked to present evidence that he or she had read:
at least twenty-five books (or equivalent);
a balance of literature and non-literary public discourse;
at least three different genres or modes;
at least five different authors;
at least four books about one issue.

Commentary

Greg's reading records from January to May indicate that his range of reading is limited (mostly horror).

Greg's teacher certified that he had read and understood the books he listed here. In addition to these reading logs, Greg demonstrated his understanding through conferences, book reports, and presentations. Greg's teacher wrote that he "completed 5 books this year for a total of 975 pages."

Greg fell far short of the requirements for the breadth of reading task.

Connections to Standards

Greg needs to show substantial improvement in:

• reading a wide range of print and nonprint texts (1);

• reading a wide range of literature (2).

3rd Quarter Reading Log

Date	Title-Author	Pages Read	Completed	Comments
Jan 19	The X-men Tom ureany : Darcy			
Jan 23	The anno Brigun Glen Larg	7-11		
Jun 24		11-16		
Jan 25		16-20		
Jan 26		21-25		
Jan 31		25-29		
Feb 1				
march 13	magic ...	1-5		
march 14		5-8		
march 15		12-18		
		18-30	✓	
3-20	Web of Horror nacykc	152p	✓	I think That was a good Book Because I Like Some Horror in Books
march 20		40-44		
march 27		44-40		

4th Quarter Reading Log

Date	Title-Author	Pages Read	Completed	Comments
march 24	2. Cstine my horresst	1-27		
march 28		27-41		
may 19		51-70		
march 30		70-78	W/5 12 total	
april 24	RL. stin Welcome to nu...	1-5		
april 25		5-10		
april 26		30-30		
april 27		41-47		
may 1		56-61		
may 3		61-64		

Task

The teacher asked students to do a research paper on a selected subject. On the entry slip for this piece Greg wrote, "Doing the research paper helped me organize my thoughts, made me learn about more sources. It made me read and wright better."

Report of Information (Description)

A.

Jesse James

Jesse Woodson James was born September 5, 1847 in Kearney, Missouri. His Parents were Robert James and Zerelda Cole James. His brother was Alexander Franklin James also Known as Frank. His father was a Baptist minister. Jesse also had a brother named Robert who died in infancy, and a sister named Susan. When Jesse was small his dad went to California to minister to

B. the gold miners a few weeks later he got sick, died and was buried in an unmarked grave. As a Child Jesse and Frank had rifles and Pistols, and became experts at using them. Jesse became an outlaw at a very young age, because of all the uprising during the civil war. The first bank robbery the James brothers did was Clay County Savings bank of Liberty on February 13 1866. Their gang consisted of Frank and Jesse, Cole, Jim and and Bob Younger, and their other bandits Bill Chadwell, Charlie Pitts, and Clel Miller. During a Bank robbery in Northfield, Missouri

C. in 1876 the town fought back and Jesse and Frank were the only ones that escaped.

They robbed numerous banks and trains and were wanted for murder and armed robbery.

D. Jesse married his cousin Zerelda mimms or zee. They had two children, Mary and Jesse Edwards, But he still continued his life of Crime.

Paper continued on page 110

R u b r i c / C o m m e n t a r y

A. Successfully uses chronological method of organization.

B. Demonstrates some control of spelling, punctuation, and usage. In fact, the work on this piece is of higher quality than the work on Greg's previous pieces.

C. Uses paragraphs to indicate change of topic.

D. Cites many facts and details about life of Jesse James.

GREG'S PORTFOLIO

Connections to Standards

Greg is developing skill in:

• gathering and synthesizing data from a variety of sources (7);

• communicating discoveries in ways appropriate to his purpose and audience (7).

During his life Jesse James was referred to by many different names. Some People called him "Robin Hood" because it was said, he would help women and children. He was also called "Bloody Bill", and the "American Bandit".

There was a $10,000 reward out for Jesse, Dead or alive, because he committed so many bank and train robberies. On April 3rd, 1882, Jesse James was shoot in the back by Bob Ford, one of their new gang members. It was believed that that: Bob Ford made a deal with Governor Crittenden to get amnesty, if he killed Jesse.

E. His tombstone read

In Loving Rememberance
Jesse W. James
aged 34 years, six months, 29 days
Murdered by a traitor and coward whose name is not worthy to appear here.

F. It is said more books have been written about Jesse James than any other outlaw ever.

Bibliography

Book with one author
Bradley, Larry. Jesse James! The making of a Legend. Nevada. Tarsin Publishers. 1980, 7-148.

Book with one Author
Settle, William. Jesse James was his name. Missouri, University of Missouri Press, 1966. pg 1-201

Task

The teacher asked students to preplan the research report. The outline and drafts were two suggestions. Greg presents an outline.

Jesse James — Out line

I. Early Life
A. Childhood
1. Jesse James was born in September 5, 1847
2. Jesse grew up on a farm in Kearney Missouri
3. Jesse was always playing with his brothers and talking about being an outlaw.

B. Family
1. Jesse dad was Rev. Robert James
2. Jesses mothers name was Zerelda Samual
3. Jesse had 4 brothers named Cole, Bob, Jim and John.

II. Adult Life
A. Nick name
1. "People all around the world called Jesse "Bloody Bill"
2. People call Jesse the worst outlaw ever.
3. Theodor Roosevelt called Jesse James Robin Hood.

B. Married Life
1. Jesse married his cousin
2. Zerelda Mimms was Jesse wife
3. Jesse had two children named marry and Jesse Edwards.

III. reasons for being famous
A. Bank Robber and outlaw
1. Jesse James robbed alot of trains, Banks, and stores.
2. Jesse and his gang robbed Iron Mountain.
3. Every day he had his gun with him

B. People thought he was a hero
1. There has been more stuff writen in the world about Jesse and his gang
2. He was called american Bandit
3. Jesse Protected helpless women and children.

Reflective Essay

Task

The teacher gave the students several choices, one being a reflective essay on learning goals.

Rubric / Commentary

A. Discusses few if any effective reading strategies.
B. Sets vague goals but does not suggest specific strategies for achieving them.

Connections to Standards

Greg needs to show substantial improvement in:

• applying a wide range of strategies to comprehend, interpret, evaluate, and appreciate texts (3).

A.
B.

I decide what I read is I look on the back of the book I get started I mostly read at night about 15 min. I read pretty good and some times I dont like to read. Most of the time I read Novel like R.L. Stine Book when I get missed up I just skip th word I dont know. I have tried to make my reading Better by reading more. My goals are that I read more write more and do alot of reading on my free time.

Summary Commentary of Greg's Portfolio

The entries in Greg's portfolio suggest that Greg needs to show substantial improvement to reach adequate levels of achievement in the English language arts. Most of the pieces are brief, the longest being the report on Jesse James. Greg has given readers of his portfolio sparse evidence on which to base their judgments of what he knows and can do.

The frequent and distracting errors in basic conventions which pervade the portfolio selections suggest that Greg has difficulty with encoding. The single, brief, superficial response to *West against the Wind* suggests that he has a limited understanding of what he reads. An exception is his report on Jesse James, which shows that Greg can interpret informational texts with some competence. However, most of the evidence presented here suggests that Greg is not a fluent reader. In writing, although he shows some fluency, Greg makes numerous and distracting errors in spelling, punctuation, and usage. The "Jesse James" report, which is practically error-free, suggests that Greg's work benefits from proofreading (although he provided no evidence of having done this).

The entries in Greg's portfolio suggest that he is not skilled in processing information and that he is not aware of strategies he might use to better understand and represent ideas. For example, in his reading reflection, he states, "When I get mixed up I just skip the word I don't know." He expresses the wish to read more and to read more skillfully, but he does not articulate any strategies for achieving these goals. In his letter of introduction, Greg states that he is "a pretty good reader writer and language user because I try good at those things." In this letter Greg also hints that he understands that his reading and writing might improve if he did more of it, but he does not state any plan for doing this.

The portfolio pieces shown here were not written for a range of close and distant audiences. Greg's "Letter to the Editor" shows confusion about purpose and audience. "The Kids with the Revolver," a topic potentially of interest to a peer audience, is a rambling account which starts and stops. The "Jesse James" report, however, shows the beginnings of an authoritative voice.

Greg does not write in a variety of forms. Most pieces are brief and unfocused with little difference in structure and style. One judge who scored Greg's portfolio wrote, "Each piece in here is the same—an expository stance—retelling or giving answers. There are no connections between texts and limited use of genres." The evidence of reading presented here suggests that Greg approaches and responds to all texts in similar (literal) fashion.

The limited evidence in Greg's portfolio does not show that he knows or understands key concepts in English. For example, in his response to *West against the Wind* his justification for identifying Abigail as the main character is that she "is in the book the most." "Most" is not carefully considered. Similarly, Greg provides no evidence of working with cultural ideas or themes.

Overall, Greg's portfolio demonstrates that he has a low level of declarative knowledge (knowing that). His reading and writing are not yet fluent. Nevertheless, the "Jesse James" report shows that Greg can produce relatively fluent and error-free texts. The lack of variety among the entries in the portfolio (even though a variety of artifacts was required by the portfolio program in which he participated) suggests that Greg's procedural knowledge (knowing how) is at a very low level. Similarly, there is little evidence to suggest that Greg has drawn on background knowledge (knowing about) in order to produce the pieces shown here. That is, Greg's lack of experience with a variety of genres of reading and writing probably contributes to the overall poor quality of his portfolio pieces.

Greg's case raises interesting questions. How can Greg be helped to consistently produce the quality of work he begins to demonstrate in the "Jesse James" report? To what strategies might Greg be introduced to help him become a better reader and writer? One judge who scored Greg's portfolio suggested, "Knowing about his process might really help this student to play to his strengths and develop some greater interest and motivation to read and write." Greg's portfolio demonstrates the low range of performance, but his work also suggests that he has an interest in becoming a more skilled reader, writer, and language user and that he has some knowledge and skills upon which to build. The key may be his engagement with topics he likes (Jesse James).

Conclusion

The *Exemplar Series* is the third part of the NCTE standards project. (1) *Standards for the English Language Arts* (NCTE/IRA); (2) the *Standards in Practice* series and the *Standards Consensus* series; and (3) the *Exemplar Series*. The aim of the *Exemplar Series* is the same as that of *Standards for the English Language Arts* (NCTE/IRA, 1996): ". . . to ensure that all students develop the literacy skills they need to succeed in school and in various areas of life" (p. 68). The exemplars and portfolios in this book are intended to make visible to all stakeholders in the educational process the kinds of tasks teachers of English language arts value, the levels of performance that frequently co-exist in a single classroom, and the criteria by which student performances are often evaluated.

It is unfortunate, but true, that many teachers of English language arts still carry on their work in isolation from a professional community and rarely see work by students other than their own. Likewise, many students in English language arts classrooms lack opportunities to study and discuss the work of other students in other classrooms and to evaluate their own performance with reference to standards and/or rubrics. The intent of this book is to put the exemplars and portfolios into the hands of those who stand to benefit most from them—teachers and students.

Three final caveats are in order. (1) Use this book to develop your own local assessment, not as a substitute for it. (2) Use this book only as a resource to develop your own course outline, not as *the* course outline. (3) Use this book to develop your own exemplars, rubrics, and commentaries. This book is *not* a scoring guide.

This book is only a bare sketch of what there is to know about the performance levels of students on the NCTE/IRA standards. The value of this book will be in the processes it generates and the discussions it inspires about what we, the English language arts teaching profession, K–12, value in student work.

EDITORS

Miles Myers received his B.A. in rhetoric, his M.A. in English and M.A.T. in English and education, and Ph.D., from the Language and Learning Division, at the University of California–Berkeley. He has served as the Executive Director of the National Council of Teachers of English since 1990, and has been president of the Central California Council of Teachers of English (in the 1960s), a vice president of the California Association of Teachers of English (in the 1970s), president of the Oakland Federation of Teachers-AFT (in the 1960s), and president of the California Federation of Teachers-AFT (in the 1980s). He was the administrative director of the Bay Area (California) and National Writing Projects during the first ten years of their development, and for almost thirty years, he has been secretary-treasurer and later president of Alpha Plus Corporation, a nonprofit corporation of preschools in Oakland, California. He taught high school English for many years, primarily at Oakland High School, where he was department chair until 1975, when he left for the University of California–Berkeley. He taught English methods courses at the University of California–Berkeley for five years, at the University of Illinois Urbana-Champaign for three years, and at various other institutions for shorter periods of time. He was co-director of the literacy unit of New Standards, and he serves on the advisory boards of the Center for the Study of Writing at the University of California–Berkeley and the National Research Center on Literature Teaching and Learning at the State University of New York at Albany, as well as the Board on Testing and Assessment of the National Academy of Science. He has received the Distinguished Service Award from the California Association of Teachers of English, the Ben Rust Award for Service from the California Federation of Teachers-AFT, and an Exemplary Service Award from the California Council of Classified Employees. He has authored six books and monographs as well as many articles on the teaching of English.

Elizabeth Spalding received her B.A. in Latin and English and M.A. in Latin from West Virginia University, and her Ph.D. in Curriculum Studies and Language Education from Indiana University-Bloomington. She is assistant professor in the Department of Curriculum and Instruction at the University of Kentucky. Previously, she was Project Manager for Standards at the National Council of Teachers of English, where she worked on the NCTE/IRA project to develop K–12 content standards and managed the New Standards project to develop performance assessment tasks and a portfolio assessment system. She has conducted numerous workshops on portfolio scoring and other assessments. She taught high school English, French, and Latin for many years in West Virginia and in the Department of Defense Dependents Schools–Pacific Region. Her research interests include teacher perspectives, teacher education, and alternative assessment of literacy. She has authored several articles on alternative assessment and the experiences of novice teachers.